# A Lucky Strike

Pablo Bohoslavsky

The right of Pablo Bohoslavsky to be identified as the author of this work has been asserted by him in accordance with the Copyright, Designs and Patents Act, 1988

Copyright ©2015 Pablo Bohoslavsky

Translator: Pascual José Masullo
Editor: Dr Robert Gurney
Cover design: William Gurney

ISBN 978-0-9932299-0-9

All rights reserved. No part of this publication may be reproduced, stored in retrieval system or transmitted in any form or by any means electronic, mechanical, photocopying, recording or otherwise, without the prior permission of the publisher, except in the case of brief quotations embodied in critical articles and reviews.

Published in the United Kingdom in 2015 by
Cambria Books, Wales, United Kingdom

# Foreword

Pablo B. has taken his time. The time needed for a hard and painful process of digestion. Because it's only now, decades later, that he revisits –rather, he allows himself to revisit- the years swallowed (because you do swallow and digest prison) in Rawson during the Dictatorship.

It has not been easy. Those years and those memories have gradually settled and been purged of fear and hatred. But, being indelible, they live on, implicit, tacit, conjured up by a sensitive and selective memory.

There arc no obscene descriptions of cruelty, no hits below the belt: horror can be left unsaid, it follows naturally, it flows between the lines in the shape of a light, chilly and continual sweat in all the scenes, through a visible trembling of hands or an audible wavering of voices, without having to be expressed in the ominous dialogues in which the possibility of death is always lurking in the background.

The proud integrity involved in writing -with shy modesty and wise reticence- these atrocious and pathetic accounts, often ironic and full of paradoxes, are as revealing of moral integrity and ethical memory as the most ferocious face-to-face denunciation of the state terrorism in Argentina responsible for torture, and crimes against humanity. Bearing names and initials that at once identify and conceal them, the characters in these stories - notes spontaneously taken apparently purporting to be anecdotes- are unforgettable. I mean that the men that enjoy this paradoxical fate - "Guys, we´re in luck. We´re going to prison"– take on a life of their own, as fully fledged characters do, beyond any specific identification or documented reference.

In these short stories we find inmates and wardens using the rhetoric characteristic of prison life, a seamless microcosm that reproduces on a smaller scale the countless possibilities of the larger extent of the Dictatorship: a dentist and a barber –sadists out of a handbook, but still with contradictions– who resemble characters in García Marquez´s stories; raving paranoids that communicate through signs; players of a ghostly chess game made up of light taps and virtual notes; dogmatic pessimists that make the most ill-omened prophecies; joyful detectors of the prisoners´ desperate hope dogged by misfortune; unshakeable cynics who find comfort in jokes and black humour as an antidote against fear and hopelessness; and even some obscure officer not yielding to barbarism and impunity, who finds a loophole to save some kind of code and an anonymous convict when checking a roster.

They are all here, evoked by the first-hand experience and recent memories of Pablo Bohoslavsky, one more time asserting "Never Again".

*Juan Sasturain, April 2010*

# A Lucky Strike

"Hey, you!" said one of the men that couldn´t be seen by the hooded prisoners. On saying this, he kicked Julio R. in the leg warning him the message was addressed to him. "Now they will take you to the lavatory, you will take a shower and shave. You will be given clean clothes, and you should be alert because you will be transferred. Got it?"

Julio R. clenched his jaws and his throat involuntarily contracted his vocal chords. "Yes sir," he managed to mutter.

Julio R. had a hunch that the fate the future had in store for him was the same as that of many *desaparecidos* in his town: to appear publicly in the media, but dead.

The invisible man walked off in a different direction. None of the kidnapped men, who were either chained to the floor or handcuffed on one of the rough beds in the room, wished to be the target of the invitation to hygiene and grooming he had just heard. Though they were in hell, they would rather stay there than start the road to death.

The man's footsteps resounded on the wood floor. For some, for those who could hear him march away, the clatter was a relief. For others, instead, the nearness of the footfalls threatened to make their hearts burst.

The invisible man repeated the ritual three more times: warning, kicking and ordering Rubén R., Agustín C., and Víctor B., just as he has done in the case of Julio R. One by one the four of them were led away to perform the preparatory ritual that would quench, albeit in infinitesimal proportions, the thirst of those earthly gods intent on saving humankind.

It was night when they made them get into a van, tied behind their backs and blindfolded. Guides helped them so they would not stumble or bump into anything. They were going to kill them, and yet, paradoxically, they didn't want to hurt them. They didn't even want them to get a scratch.

The van drove for an hour. Then for another hour. It drove around as if looking for the right spot. Finally the driver stopped the van. The invisible man led the men in the dark.

The four men could feel the gravel under their feet and smell recently mown grass. It was November, in late spring. The birds chirped, announcing daylight. A few sparrows on the lower branches, *benteveos* (great Kiskadees) on the higher ones, *corbatitas* (seed eaters) darting by invisibly, and the indefatigable *horneros* (oven birds) made up a farewell choir. Julio R. was familiar with the geography of the place. He thought: "This is Parque de Mayo."

They made the four men stand shoulder to shoulder until the square was closed. Julio R., Rubén R, Agustín C. and Victor B. believed this was their last daybreak. Some said goodbye mentally, others felt contrite, all of them cursed. None of them begged for mercy, not even when they heard the order: "Now get down on your knees." The birds seemed to be chirping more loudly; Victor B. remembered the quote from Chekhov his younger brother Andy would repeat: "Blackbirds roar in Russia," and concluded: "These common sparrows do that."

One of the invisible men said: "Gentlemen, now count to one hundred. Then take off your blindfolds, untie your hands, and go home. If you dare report this event or go back to politics, you will be dead meat." The four men heard the van doors open and close. They also heard that the other three or four get into the back of the vehicle. Someone started the engine and the vehicle drove off.

Julio R., Rubén R, Agustín C. and Víctor B. stood paralysed again, by the smell of near death before, and now by this happy ending. Happy ending or trap? They didn't even dare uncover their eyes or untie their hands.

Suddenly they heard a blaring siren approaching; then a screeching halt and other invisible men running towards them; afterwards orders and a voice saying: "Please help these young men. It looks like they were going to kill them. Take off their blindfolds and untie them. They should get into our van."

It was an F-350 from the Argentine Army. When the four men recovered their sight, their eyes hurting from the morning brightness, they noticed they were driving with young officers and petty officers. One of them emphasised that they had saved their lives. "You were going to be killed. Those guys were from the Triple A; we can't follow them because we have only one vehicle." The four men agreed with a light nod, without uttering a word.

Then came the usual questions followed by cautious answers:

"Where were you?"

"We don't know," they said, although they knew they had been on grounds of the Army Fifth Corps in Bahía Blanca, less than a mile from where they had been left.

"Did they torture you?"

"No," was the answer, although the pain they felt in their bodies and minds, which they would feel for years to come, was already there.

They finally got to the headquarters of that military unit. When the F-350 stopped, the four of them, having been politely asked to get out, saw opposite them a true military parade: A general, colonels, as well as petty officers arrayed according to rank, were scrutinising them with suspicion.

General V. spoke first, addressing the four of them: "Gentlemen, we have rescued you from a paramilitary group that attempted to kill you. You should be grateful to the efficient patrolling of officers and petty officers of our Argentine army for saving your lives. Do you have any identification on you?"

"No sir," the four men replied in unison.

"Let me tell you in advance that you will be detained here until your personal situation is cleared up. We want to know if you have any record relating to subversion or if you have committed any crime against persons or property. If you do, you will be tried by a military court, if you don't you will be set free."

The four of them gave a light nod again.

Then V. asked: "Do you have any family or friends in Bahía Blanca?"

The four men answered, excited and in unison: "Yes, sir."

"You are allowed to make a phone call each. Let your family know that you are well, and that they can come and visit you. However, as I said before, be forewarned that you can be sentenced if you have been up to any shady activities. Have a good day."

"Thank you very much, sir," the four of them inadvertently agreed.

Each of the men made a mental effort to remember the telephone number of someone they would not compromise if they called them, while Agustín C., feeling reassured and willing to cheer up the other three, uttered, curiously enough, words that sounded like a life-song, like a desirable near future: "Hey boys, we are in luck. We´re going to jail."

# Good Fellows

"We have a lot to thank you for, Mr. Vice-Chancellor. Your institution's support has made it possible for these inmates, who are receiving their graduation diplomas today, to be reinstated into society much better equipped, once they have completed their sentences. You can be assured they are good fellows."

"It's the least we can do for those who desire a future different from the hard present they have to live in. Besides, that prisoners should want to further their education may stand as a genuine example for other correctional establishments. I hope they will follow us."

It was the year 1995. Pedro B., Vice-Chancellor of an institution of higher education, and Adalberto G., governor of a unit in the Federal Penitentiary Service, were exchanging those words at a ceremony meant to reward the effort made by some inmates who had successfully completed their university education.

The hall was packed with journalists who wanted to cover an original and hopeful event in comparison with those usually associated with prisons: break-out attempts, squalor, abuse, human rights violations. It was a sort of roofed playground where the inmates did physical exercise: tiled floor, spectator stands on one side, painted stripes marking the boundaries of the basketball and soccer fields. The hoops and the goal iron posts rested on one side.

The ceremony was attended by some of the town's political authorities, as well as the diocesan bishop and the chaplain. Pedro B. was in the company of two assistants and the prison's Governor wore his best uniform. Both the Mayor and the other officials present were also ceremoniously dressed up.

There were refreshments on the tables covered with white tablecloths, some new, others old and yellowish. The guests could drink white or red wine, sodas or water, from glasses which glittered in the sunlight thanks to the efforts of those who had washed them again and again so they would look better.

The inmates with the best conduct record were in charge of the catering. They moved around politely and silently among the guests and authorities, replenishing the glasses and making sure there were enough hors d´oeuvres and sandwiches on the plates. The three graduating inmates enjoyed their peers' exceptional attention. After all, they had had to put up with all kinds of abuse and outrages from the same authorities. "It's the new policy," was the only explanation they could come up with.

The soft canned music in the background completed the picture. Some party! The occasion certainly called for it.

Adalberto G. was brimming with joy, and insisted on the virtues of the academic initiative he was responsible for. He was also celebrating his new appointment as Governor. The wine seemed to have helped him unwind. He was chirpy and eager to chat with his guests.

"If you will allow me, Mr. Vice-Chancellor, I would like to tell you something."

"By all means, Mr. Governor."

"After so many years of struggling for better conditions for the inmates, this is a great victory."

"I can imagine. Have you been in the penitentiary service for too long?"

"Almost thirty years. I started in 1966, during Ongania´s presidency. I have worked here under constitutional as well as *de facto* governments. But mind you, I never changed the way I treated my inmates."

"It's been very noble of you to uphold your principles in the face of adversity."

"I have no doubt. I have always been inspired by a desire to help convicts to go back into society. I have worked in institutions where the inmates had been convicted, even after appealing. I can't say that they were like my own sons, but I have always thought they could all be reclaimed for society, and that they deserved another chance."

"Sure. Is that why you call them good fellows?"

"Ah! So you have realised, haven't you?" Some show surprise when I call them that. But that is how I see them. Look, it may seem exaggerated, but I have taken it upon myself as something akin to a redemption task. Almost like a priesthood. Well, that must be the reason why I never married or had any children. Now that we have a democratic government, I feel much more at ease with this responsibility I have taken upon my shoulders."

Pedro B. was flabbergasted. Very few knew that he himself had been in the Rawson Prison in those years. He didn't hide it, of course he didn't, although he didn't boast either about his passage through the southern prison. After all, he used to say it was an involuntary passage. And besides, he had shared his misfortune with thousands of others, between 1976 and 1983.

However, what struck him as odd was the enthusiasm and vocation shown by the prison governor. He had even used the words *redemption task, priesthood.* "Quite a definition, although a little exaggerated," he thought to himself.

Adalberto G. looked vaguely familiar to him. Maybe they had met a few years before. He reasoned: "I was in prison in Rawson, he entered the service in 1966... , perhaps we did run across each other." This thought encouraged him.

"Governor, I'm just curious. You say you entered the service some thirty years ago, is that right?"

"Yes, that's right. I´ve had a long career. But I will retire soon, I think, as I deserve. Why do you ask?"

"Because you look familiar to me. Maybe we have seen each other sometime before."

"That's quite likely. I have been in so many institutions. By the way, what's your field?"

"History."

"Maybe that's the connection."

The journalists covering the event came up to them, eager to interview Adalberto G. about his job in the penitentiary service during the last dictatorship. Maybe he had something interesting to tell them. So they didn't hesitate to approach him, taking advantage of the happy circumstance that had brought them together, as well as the casual atmosphere of the event.

"Mr. Governor, I´m from the newspaper *La Semana Austral.* We see that you are a man concerned about his prisoners. Why don't you tell us about your job and activities during the military process?"

"Sure, I was in Villa Devoto for a while, then in Ezeiza, a while in Rawson. But my ultimate goal, as I was saying before to the Vice-Chancellor here, has always been for prisoners to become useful citizens again, and serve society after completing their term in prison."

"You will excuse me, sir, but in those years prisoners were abused, they were not even allowed to read. Some were even removed from prison to be taken away and then killed mercilessly."

"Sure, I can't deny that, but I repeat: I was only moved by the desire to re-educate prisoners for society, so I have always worked towards that goal."

The journalists exchanged glances. No one asked any more questions. There followed a deathly silence, which lasted a few minutes. Adalberto G. thought that if he didn't clear things up, the journalists would have good reason to call his good record into question.

"And let me tell you, dear journalists. I wasn't bald as I am now. I had a thick head of red hair back then. And guess what nickname the inmates used to call me by, as a token of their friendship and closeness, especially those who had been arrested for political reasons. He didn't wait for their answer, as they didn't know it. They used to call me, behind my back, of course, *el ruso G.*, or *red G.*"

When he heard this, Pedro B. felt he was before a revelation. He opened his eyes wide and his memory went back several years, only to immediately bring back fragments of his past. "Now I can place him," he said to himself.

"Mr. Governor, now I *do* remember where we met."

"Indeed? Where do you remember me from?"

"From Rawson, sir. I was there between the years 1977 and 1981."

The journalists couldn't believe their ears. They didn't know whether this was a real scoop, or mere chance information.

"Really? What a coincidence!"

"Indeed, quite a coincidence! Almost twenty years have passed, and if you hadn't mentioned the nickname, I wouldn't have recognised you."

"Oh, boy!" So you taught history there. That's quite praiseworthy."

"No. I was just one of your good fellows."

"Adalberto G. started to feel ill at ease. His face gradually went red, doing justice to his old nickname."

"I think I was the administration chief in those days."

"No, Governor. You should remember. You were the prison's internal security chief."

A strained snicker could be heard. "What a good memory you have! And you still remember those years? You would rather forget them, surely."

"You know what? I couldn't forget them, even if I wanted to. You see, there is always one of your good fellows around you."

"Mr Governor, please, don't feel bad about this. After all, you managed to reclaim me for the good of society. If you don't mind, I will now tell the journalists how you succeeded in doing so."

# The Human Body: a Perfect Machine

"It looks like I'm going, after all," thought Pedro B. as he read the notice in front of the gate. He was being informed that on April 15, 1981, he would have served his sentence and would be released from the Rawson Penitentiary. He was a mere twenty-four hours away from that day.

His wife had already given him the nod, but even so his legs shook at the official notice. He looked pale and could hardly move.

"Bad news, inmate?," asked the officer on duty, almost willing it to be so.

"No, sir. Just the opposite"

He took a deep breath, turned his back on the iron bars he was to go through in a few hours, closed his eyes for an instant, and headed for the first desk between the two wings of the building. He sank down and silently produced his imminent release notice for whoever was willing to read it.

A whisper travelled from mouth to mouth, like a soft autumn breeze, unusual in Patagonia, loaded with envy, joy, and wishes of multiplication: "Pedro B. is leaving."

"I've been in prison almost five years, four of them in Rawson, and here I am, in one piece, well, almost in one piece." He looked around.

"Some of the inmates are screwed-up," Pedro B. thought to himself and, in order to strengthen his point of view, he added "Juan Carlos, who comforts and encourages those who have lost all hope, spends the whole time in front of the building gate asking if any member of his family has come for a visit. He does it every day, methodically, once in the morning, once in the afternoon and then again before close-up. For the last two months he had not been summoned for the long-awaited encounter."

He went on: "Honorio, once a great reader and talker, is always quiet. He used to write letters for the illiterate prisoners who had ended up in the Rawson Penitentiary: those young men, still teenagers, who had been rounded up during the raids in the Tucumán Forest in 1975 and 1976. Honorio was such an avid reader, he would devour whatever he could lay his hands on: censored newspapers and magazines as well as authorised novels. He would read, discuss and comment on his own readings as well as others'. He had an exceptionally reflexive and analytical mind. He now spends his hours on his rough bed, rocking in an imaginary chair and gazing at the line where the wall meets the ceiling."

Pedro B. stood up and walked up to Juan Carlos. He took him by the arm and whispered in his ear as affectionately as he could: "My friend, you have got to realise you will be duly notified of a family visit. Don't work yourself up. We all want to see our loved ones."

Juan Carlos H. stared at him.

"I get close to the gate just in case. What if someone has come to see me, but these guys forget to let me know?"

"That could never happen, Juan Carlos. The visitors would insist."

"It's easy for you to say so. I've heard you are being released. You don't care about visits anymore. Now leave me alone."

Juan Carlos H. akwardly shook off Pedro B's arm and though he did not walk up to the gate, he looked towards it insistently, hoping.

The wardens, like sharks smelling blood, had detected in Juan Carlos H. that confusion between desire and reality. Sometimes, when the watchmen patrolled the building, walking among the prisoners, they would prod him: "I thought I heard your name. Maybe you have a visitor."

Pedro B. was perplexed. He did not expect such a blunt attitude from his mate. He confirmed: "He is not well."

He was snatched from his perplexity by Carlos V.: "Honorio would like to congratulate you," he said. Pedro B. walked up to his cell. Just when he was coming in, Honorio signed to him. It was the hospital sign of a nurse with her right index finger just above her lips, requesting silence. He sat next to him.

Honorio T. spoke to him in sign language, with rapidly moving hands, like a magician's: "Do-not-say-anything-there-are-microphones-all-over-the-cell-I-am-very-happy-that-you-are-being-set-free."

Pedro B. replied in a similar fashion: "Thank-you-but-what-makes-you-think-that-we-prisoners-have-hidden-mikes-in-our-cells?"

"Not-all-of-us-only-those-that-can-give-or-receive-important-information."

He then raised his hand, requesting with an imperative gesture that Pedro B. follow the course of his finger pointing to different spots on the walls and the ceiling. But Pedro B. could only see wrinkles, small cracks, damp patches or fly-shit in the spots Honorio T. was pointing out.

Honorio T. shook him, while at the same time asking him with a sudden wave of his right hand: "Did-you-see-the-mikes-I-pointed-out-to-you?" Pedro B. barely managed to answer, carefully picking his words: "I-can-not-see-very-well-I-am-not-wearing-my-glasses-and-it-is-already-getting-dark."

Pedro B. felt torn: while he wanted to hug Honorio T., he also wanted to leave the cell. A warden stopped in front of the cell door: "What are you doing in this cell? It's not yours, inmate."

"I apologise, Mr. Warden. I just came to say goodbye because I've been notified of my release from prison tomorrow."

"You will bid your farewell when the time comes. Get out! Can't you see that inmate T. doesn't want to talk to anyone?"

"Yes, sir. So long, Honorio."

Night fell. The prisoners had supper and were then locked up in their cells. The padlocks clicked shut with a jarring sound. The sharp click was repeated as many times as there were occupied cells. One, two, three, four… thirty-four, thirty-five, thirty-six. The wing was full. All the cells were locked. Everything was under control.

Pedro B. took a long time to go to sleep. He heard screams in the middle of the night. Though they were not unusual, a male nurse had come into the prison at the request of one of the wardens. One of the cell doors was opened.

Pedro B. was overcome with emotion at the proximity of his release and the pain caused by the realisation that two of his prison mates had entered a paranoia tunnel.

The next day, Pedro B. noticed that the building looked different, not only because he was being set free – for which he had prepared by gathering his few belongings and leaving behind some victuals for his mates, but also because he could sense something was wrong. Honorio T.'s cell, unlike all the others, stayed shut until mid-morning. About ten the warden on duty opened it, stood under the frame and called out to Pedro B.

"Honorio T. hurt himself last night. He's calm now, but has asked to see you. You have five minutes to talk."

"Thank you, sir."

The warden moved over, so that as Pedro B. walked into the cell, he could see Honorio T. with a bandage on his head and a thicker one on his abdomen.

"What's wrong with you?"

Honorio T. sat on his bed and like the day before he made his imperative silence sign with his index finger. His hand spoke again: "You-were-right-the-mikes-were-not-hidden-in-the-cell."

Pedro B. replied in the same way: "Why-can´t-we-speak-then?   And-whatever-happened-to-you?   Why-those-bandages?"

Honorio T. waved his hand: "Because-now-the-mikes-are-inside-my-body-I-tried-to-remove-them-from-my-head-and-my-stomach-that-is-why-I-hurt-myself."

Pedro B. instinctively gave Honorio a strong hug. They stayed like this until the warden looked into the cell. "Inmate, the five minutes are out."

"That's right, sir. I'm leaving right now."

Pedro B. put his hands on Honorio T.'s shoulders and barely managed to say: "Be strong." Honorio T. signed again to hush him and smiled as Pedro B. walked out of the cell.

Before midday a voice thundered from the gate: "Pedro B., get ready to leave." The time had come. He said goodbye to each one of the inmates that walked up to him giving them tight hugs. Each one of the mates had something to say, so did Pedro B., trying to comfort those who would be inexorably left behind.

When he was approaching the main gate, ready to walk through it, Juan Carlos H. caught up with him. "I'm sorry about yesterday. Can I ask you a favour?"

"Yes, man, of course."

"If you happen to find my family outside, please tell them I'm getting ready to go to the visit room, and that I'm very happy they have come to see me."

"Sure. Cheer up!"

# Mr. Alejo

He finally arrived. The warden Isidoro G. took several walks around Rawson in order to understand what inmate Juan Z. had told him. That October spring in 1980 found him wearing his heavy boots and his winter work-clothes. Isidoro G.´s female workmates were the first to demand a change in his wardrobe. "They´re out of season," was the argument they put forth.

He walked down Antartic Argentina Avenue for a while towards the mouth of the Chubut River. The afternoon sun was quite strong, but stronger still was his determination to decipher the words spoken to him by Juan Z.: "The waters battle with each other." This funny expression brought a light smile on his face. "Like two boxers," he thought.

Everything had started one day when Isidoro G. had walked past Juan Z., who was sitting on his cell bed and, leaning across the table built into the wall, was reading a book, all wrapped up in his thoughts. His right forefinger ran along the lines, guiding him. He was so engrossed with his reading that he was taken aback by Isidoro G.'s words: "What are you reading, inmate?"

"A novel, Mr. Warden."

"What is it about, if you don't mind my asking?"

"It's about how men change according to circumstances. Those that appear to be good are not so good, and those that appear to be evil are not so evil. We sometimes do things that make us proud, but sometimes we do things that we are ashamed of."

"Do you say that with regard to me, inmate?"

"No, Mr. Warden. I mean in general, but it nearly always applies to all human beings."

Silence fell. As no more questions were asked of Juan Z., he excused himself and resumed his reading. Isidoro G. was still standing in the doorway, pondering.

"At least now you are allowed to read. Things are not so bad as they were two or three years ago."

"Things are better for me too. They no longer put pressure on us to punish inmates by leaving them without their food or by banning visits and cigarettes," he thought, and continued on his beat.

He walked around the wing looking into the cells where some inmates were reading books just like Juan Z., or letters, like Juan Carlos R. Everybody knew that he always read the same letter, over and over again, though he had not received any mail for a year now.

He also stood behind the tables where some inmates were talking about the daily news, others were teaching

History, Economics, or Mathematics or were simply discussing the content of the mail they had received. He looked on out of mere curiosity. He listened, he didn't spy.

Gone were the days when he had to eavesdrop on the inmates´ conversations and report their content to his superiors. Unlike other wardens, he had not enjoyed doing that. The other wardens, instead, had relished it, since it often earned them a pat on the shoulder or brought punishment upon some inmate. "Or, rather, caused great *suffering* in some inmate," he corrected himself.

But he was not among those. No. He did not long for his superiors´ recognition, nor was he a sadist, a word whose definition he had to look up in the dictionary as he heard one of the prisoners utter it.

He did one more round and then stopped in front of Juan Z.'s cell, who was still deep in his reading.

"Is that a good book, inmate? You seem to be enjoying it."

"Yes, very interesting. Do you like reading yourself?"

"Yes, I do, when I have the time. But only a little. I am not up to reading many pages in a row. You know, I was not encouraged to read as a child. I had to drop out of school when I was fifteen in order to help my dad in the fields. He then added, as if taking him into his confidence: "My family is from Corrientes, there were six of us, and we all did our share of work as children."

"It's never too late to read books, though. Several prisoners here have read books for the first time ever."

"Perhaps." The conversation was now extending a little more than was advisable.

"See you later, inmate."

"See you later, Mr. Warden."

Isidoro G. did yet one more round and walked past Juan Z.'s cell.

"Mr. Warden. Just one moment, please."

"Yes?"

"I took the liberty to copy out three paragraphs for you. If you like them, I can then pass the book on to you, so you can read it." He made to stand up to give him the piece of paper.

"Just hold on, inmate"

Isidoro G. looked at the gate at the end of the wing. He made sure no one was looking in his direction. He stretched out his arm into the cell and Juan Z put a small piece of paper in his hand. Isidoro G. didn´t want to find out where the pencil, or the paper on which Juan Z had left furrows of threaded words, had come from.

Isidoro G. crumpled the paper into a ball and put it in his pocket. Before resuming his nightwatch he heard Juan Z tell him: "I strongly recommend that you read it at the mouth of the Chubut River. You will see that the waters battle with each other." Make sure you do it in broad daylight."

Isidoro G. had walked almost two hours. It was four in the afternoon and he was already on a small promontory at the mouth of the river. He sat on a rock, loosened the laces of his heavy boots and his jacket collar, and wiped the sweat on his forehead.

He then pulled the crumpled paper out of his pocket. He looked on both sides. He was all by himself. He read: "The waters met. The freshwater struggled to flow out, while the seawater stopped it. The sea waves attempted to flow in and the freshwater calmly stopped it."

It was true. It was there before his own eyes. "Why didn´t I realise this before?" The river waters are meek, but they don´t easily surrender, while the seawater never ceases to insist. Its waves keep coming back. They even differed in colour and the ways in which each tried to invade the other: the seawater was gray and looked like a battering ram, while the river water looked like a balloon attempting to grow in the sea.

Isidoro G. had never taken notice of anything like this before. He didn´t even remember having it before his eyes. Brought up in the country amid farm animals, knives and ropes, he had seen the sea for the first time when he was taken for his training to Tres Arroyos, which was near a beach whose name he couldn´t remember. Now, in the summer, he would often go to Union Beach, though he didn´t like it very much. He had never paid any attention to the Chubut River, even less to its junction with the sea, as Juan Z had suggested. He went on reading: "In less than ten years, in the belief I was the master of my fate, I was led by others, by 'those' that make us and destroy us." He stopped reading. He remembered the last ten years of this life, which almost coincided with his career as penitentiary agent. "I thought I would end up doing something else, a job like any other, but I was forced to punish people by 'those' whose faces we never see."

He set his eyes on the last lines he had not yet read: "To the dead, we should add those living corpses that were the men with broken lives, with a frustrated calling, that would forever lead wretched lives, when they had not had the strength to commit suicide." Alejo C.

He had noticed that too. Some of his workmakes were men without any desire to fight. He had heard some talk about unhappiness, diseases brought about by the pain inflicted on the prisoners, about broken families and ashamed children who concealed their parents´ jobs.

Something similar could be seen among the prisoners. In his routine walks, he had noticed that some had let themselves go; they ate meagrely, had no initiative of their own, hardly ever spoke, let alone received family visits.

"Oh, my God! It´s almost six o´clock. I have spent two solid hours here."

He laced up his heavy boots, buttoned up his jacket and retraced his steps. He lived in one of the houses near the Rawson Prison, which he shared with other wardens, all of them single.

After his day off, he returned to work. Since, for security reasons, he wasn´t always assigned to the same wing, he had to wait for a week before returning to Juan Z.´s wing.

When the day arrived, he realised his heart was beating fast. He was going to speak to Juan Z, who had promised to lend him the book.

He walked into the wing, but, against his will, didn´t walk straight to Juan Z´s cell. Instead, he walked around the wing in the opposite direction. That enabled him to see him from a distance: he was reading. He walked up to the wall at the end, stopped half-way as all the wardens usually did, looked in the direction of the front gate and walked on.

He stopped before the cell gate.

"Good morning, inmate"

"Good morning, Mr Warden." "Were you able to read what I gave you?"

"Yes, that man is very good with words." He threads them very well.

"I think so."

"You said I could borrow the book from you. Is that right?"

"Well, something´s come up. They searched my room, and when they found out the author was Cuban, they confiscated it. I´m really sorry."

"May I have the title? Perhaps I can get hold of it."

"Of course! The book´s title is *El siglo de las luces* (*)."

"It said Alejo C. on the last line. What does that mean?"

"Ah! It´s the author´s name. Alejo, Alejo Carpentier."

"Thank you, inmate!"

"You´re welcome, Mr Warden!"


(*) Translator´s note: In its English version, the title of Alejo Carpentier´s masterpiece *El Siglo de las Luces* (literally, *The Century of Lights*) is *Explosion in a Cathedral*.

# A Mother's Determination

"Your son has been punished, madam. You can't see him," said the officer at the Visitors' Reception Office, full of family members who, every forty-five days or so, attempted to see one of the inmates in the Rawson prison.

"But I have come a long way, sir. I have travelled more than five hundred miles. No one told me I wouldn't be able to see Pedro."

"The thing is he infringed a rule yesterday, so they inform me from the Governor's Office, and the rules are clear: If an inmate has committed an offence, family visits are banned."

Sofía took a deep breath and sighed heavily. "Oh, my God!" And she sat right in front of the prison guard. She had been told about other cases, but this was the first time it had happened to her. What she did know, though, was that when the time approached for prisoners to get a visit, some prison guards would set them up, so it would appear they had broken a rule. No matter how small the offence, contact with family members was automatically forbidden.

In those cases no mail could be sent or received, either, and visits were suspended for a certain period of time, depending on how serious the offence was. In the case of Pedro B, this suspension lasted a whole week, exactly the length of time Sofía was able to stay in Rawson.

Pedro B. saw it coming when the guard stood at the cell gate. Rather, he had a gut feeling he was in for trouble. But he fell for it like a raw beginner, which made him all the more furious and powerless.

He knew his mother was already on her way and that she would get to the prison to see him the following day. For a long time now he had behaved, never responding to any taunts or answering back. But it was all useless.

"What are you doing, inmate?"

"I'm reading, sir." He stood up, put the book on the granite counter, put his hands behind his back and stood right there in front of the guard.

"Look at the state your bed is in! Can't you see it's a mess?"

"Well, I was sitting on it when you came in. I don't have anywhere else to sit. We don´t have any chairs, sir."

"Don't get smart with me! And stop looking at me like that! You will be punished for this."

Pedro B. couldn't believe it. He was mad with anger, realising he was already doomed.

"But you can't do this to me. I'm expecting a visit."

"You should have been more careful then. You just can't be rude to me." The guard slammed the cell gate shut, put on the padlock and headed toward the ward gate.

From there he shouted through the bars to the warden on the other side, loudly enough for the other inmates in the hall to hear: "Inmate Pedro B. in ward 3, cell 18 has been disciplined for keeping his place untidy and for being disrespectful to a prison guard. I am requesting seven days of total reclusion in his cell. Please inform the Chief Warden and the Governor."

Pedro B. heard too. "Damn! This is going to break the old woman´s heart," he thought.

But Sofía was not one to give up so easily. In fact, none of the mothers that made it to Rawson admitted defeat at the first stroke.

"And how long does this punishment last?" she asked.

"For seven days as of yesterday. He is locked up in his cell for committing two minor offences."

It was impossible for her to stay an extra week. She had left her small son, Vladimir, in a neighbour's care. Besides, she couldn't afford to neglect her clothes selling, since, although she had flexible hours, she had learned from bitter experience that she couldn't make enough to make ends meet unless she put in an effort. So spending more money on an extra week of room and board in Rawson was out of the question.

"So no chance I´ll be able to see my son?"

"No, madam. Those are the rules, and rules are to be obeyed."

"Always?" asked Sofía, trying to find a loophole.

"Always, no exceptions." answered the officer, unruffled and almost self-satisfied.

Then he added: "If you could kindly leave, I will appreciate it. You are compromising me and, besides, there are several other visitors waiting in line."

"But who can concede an exception to the visit rules? Because exceptions *have* been made," hazarded Sofia, taking a shot at it.

"Yes, but only the officer in charge of weekly visits has the authority to do so, madam."

"Well, in that case, I'm staying here until he can see me. I suppose you will not shove me off the chair, or dare to pull me up from it. I'm an older woman, in case you haven´t noticed." The officer went off to get the visits officer and briefly explained the situation to him. "That lady is here to see her son, Pedro B., but since he has been confined in this cell that privilege has been denied him. I have tried to explain to her, but she is sitting there, stopping me from helping other visitors, and she says she is not leaving until you have considered her case."

"Another fucking old woman," thought the officer. "OK, let´s go and see," he said heading for the hall, where inmates´ relatives were showing their IDs, waiting to be called to the booth. The by now five yard line kept growing behind Sofia, who still sat on the chair right across from the officer's desk.

Some fifteen minutes had already passed and the waiting visitors were beginning to get uneasy and annoyed. The visits officer thought: "That's all I need now: Family members kicking up a row so we make the headlines."

He took the officer's place and introduced himself to Sofia: "Good morning, madam. I'm the officer in charge of family members coming to see an inmate. Could you come along, please?" He wanted her out of the place at once, so that the reception process would go on smoothly, and so that he could tell her in private what the other visitors were not supposed to hear.

Sofia stood up, not without difficulty. She felt a heavy weight on her, greater than that imposed by her age. The officer walked beside her, opened a door and signalled to her to walk in and take a seat.

"I'm so sorry, madam, but regulations for subversive criminals ban visits when a prisoner has committed an offence. And your son *has* committed an offence.

"To begin with, my son is not a criminal, let alone a subversive one. But I will let that pass. I know you sometimes trick prisoners into doing something that can appear as an offence, or you just make one up, so you can prohibit visits. Besides, I can't stay a week longer. I sell clothes to support my family. I have a small son who needs me.

"Look, madam. It's none of my business how you manage to make a living. Besides, what you say about guards deliberately setting up prisoners is an utter lie, and if an inmate breaks a rule, he must be punished. There is no other way to keep order.

"Do you have a mother, sir?

"Yes, madam. Why do you ask?"

"Can you imagine how she would feel if she wanted to see you but wasn't allowed to?"

The officer remembered how many times his mother had gone to see him while he was a student at the Penitentiary Service Academy and she would go back without having seen him because he had been punished. "That should teach him how to be a man," they would tell her. At one time or another he had been able to make out from the window of his room his mother walking away, her head bent, after her visit had been denied. And he had wept each time. Bitterly. Now, instead, he was smiling before this resolute woman who was goading him relentlessly. "But before that, I should be in prison, which I´m not, unlike your son." Sofía insisted: "But it could happen to anyone. Neither my son nor I ever imagined that I should pay him a visit in a prison, but look now! Besides he is not even getting a fair trial."

She added: "It could even happen to one of your children. Do you have grown-up children, officer?" He felt he was on shaky ground. "A twenty-one-year-old daughter and a nineteen-year-old son."

"Well then, were one of them to be arrested, fairly or unfairly, wouldn't you want to bring them your affection?"

"That's for sure, but I can't do it here. If I allow you, then other visitors will request that I make an exception too."

Sofía rested her hands on the edge of the desk and leaned over it. "Look here, I will not breathe a word. I won't even tell my son. Anyway, don't expect me to be grateful to you. You should instead think about your mother and your children. Misfortune can hit anyone," she concluded, gazing into the officer's eyes. They remained in silence for thirty seconds. The officer put his right elbow on the desk and cupped his hand under his chin. "This woman is right to some extent, even if her son is a terrorist. And you never know what life has in store for you," he thought. He remembered officer Benítez, whose son had been arrested for a crime that his father swore, to whoever was willing or unwilling to listen to him, that he had nothing to do with. They had framed him just to screw him. Benítez travelled to Sierra Chica every two months to see his boy sentenced to life imprisonment for supposedly killing a policeman. "Oh, fuck!" He thought.

"All right, madam, follow me. You will see your son. But not a word about this. Got it?"

"OK." They walked back to the visitors' hall side by side. He put his hand on the officer at the reception desk´s shoulder.

"Officer, this lady has special permission from me to see his son. Admit her. She´s been waiting for quite a while. I'll sign the memo later."

"Yes, sir. This way, madam. Come with me." He stood up and spoke into the intercom. "Instruct Pedro B. in ward 3, cell 18 to get ready for a visit." One could almost hear the guard at the gate of ward 3 clench his teeth and then thunder: "Inmate Pedro B., get ready for a visit." Pedro B. heard it, but he thought it was a mistake. He remembered that sometimes they would mix up the prisoners´ names on purpose, just to give them a hard time.

The warden opened the gate. "Come on, move it. Don't keep us waiting."

Pedro B. walked down several hallways, his hands behind his back, while the gates first opened and then shut behind him with a clank. They were leading him by the arm at a brisk pace, almost at a trot. He would have preferred to run, though. They finally showed him into the visitors' hall and sat him at the barred window.

His mother, like all the other mothers, fathers, spouses, significant others, sons and daughters, brothers and sisters, aunts and uncles, cousins, was sitting on the other side of a thick glass panel that prevented any physical contact. Communication was through a microphone, and guards standing on either side could hear the conversation over a loudspeaker.

They sat Pedro B. opposite his mother, who was eagerly waiting for him, her face stuck to the glass and her arms folded.

"Mom, what a nice surprise! I thought I would not be allowed to see you for breaking a rule yesterday."

"Oh, God! As if I didn't suffer enough already from your imprisonment. I insisted a little bit."

"As simple as that?"

"All right, no more questions. So, how are you doing?"

# Urinary Healings

"Piss is very good for chilblains. You have to rub your hands with it. Let them get well impregnated, and then rub your feet with them. The trick is done: the itching goes away, your toes and instep are no longer swollen, and the chilblains never come back," said Bernardo J.

The other inmates gazed at him, some sceptical, others credulous. The cold weather in Rawson wreaked havoc with most of the prisoners' health in a prison without heating.

The conversation in Ward 6, around one of the tables in the middle, went on smoothly with remarks on the recommended potions that were handy, and on the signals from the outside world that reached the prison. The conclusions they would draw were the most ludicrous you can imagine.

The decoding of certain smells that wafted in through the gates, combined with a dubious exercise in statistical inference, and foreshadowed the next menu: "That smells like roasted beef. Besides, it's been a while since we last ate some, and it's Sunday to boot. I think we are in luck today," argued Pedro V.

"Does the thing about piss work? Or is it a joke?" asked Alberto T. As a newcomer, he was unaware of the codes shared by the other inmates, and so did not want to be the butt of ridicule by attempting to get rid of the chilblain on one of his feet with the urine prescription recommended by Bernado J.

"We all do it here as soon as winter sets in. And it never fails. So, young man, you should be neither afraid nor ashamed," added Mario C. encouragingly. He was an advanced medical student, a *Peronist* activist who had been kidnapped together with his brother. He combined a permanent disposition to comfort the weak with a subtle irony which, for those who knew him, helped to cheer them up. His knowledge of medicine had been helpful in more than one emergency, and his diagnoses used to be confirmed by the doctors in the penitentiary.

"Against common belief, urine is not waste. It doesn't come from the intestines, but through a blood filter of a similar nature to that of blood whey or to that of amniotic liquid." He went on, "It can even be drunk in extreme situations. If we drink just a little we can survive, except when being tortured. Some have drunk it as soon as they had the chance in order to commit suicide."

Several inmates looked at Mario C. in astonishment. He expatiated on the healing properties of human piss as well as the advantages and harm its use or consumption could bring about.

Sunday was a good day for these meetings. There were no visits, letters could neither be received nor written, and the prisoners were not subjected to inspections or surprise transfers either. It was also a holiday for the penitentiary staff, or a truce, rather.

Besides, this Sunday afternoon without soccer seemed endless.

They all remained thoughtful, but Mario C. prodded further: "You must have heard the saying that getting pissed on by dogs is like a bad omen. However, when you get pissed on by a human being, it's exactly the opposite. Victor J. challenged him: "Come off it, you liar. Where did you pull that one from?"

"From personal experience. It is not enough to postulate a law, but it happens over and over again."

"And how did it happen?"

"I'll tell you if you do not interrupt me," challenged Mario C., making eye contact with his mates. They had all rested their elbows on the table now, intrigued by the case. A mystery had been created.

"C'mon, no one is going to interrupt you. But don't bullshit us, you tend to exaggerate."

"I had been kidnapped. As you know, I was an active member of the *unidad básica* in Berisso. There was a raid while we were having a meeting, and they picked us up. We had been thrown together like animals, actually, worse than animals. Blindfolded and tied to a pole, we were beaten, tortured by electric shock and threatened all the time. I lost track of time, but I'm sure this went on for over two weeks."

"And did you piss in your pants?" asked Lucio M.

"Yes, several times. We also shat in our pants, when it couldn't be helped. When we had to go, we insistently asked, and even begged to be taken out, at least to the yard outside. They would grant us that favour on very few occasions."

"And did pissing in your pants help at all?" insisted Lucio M.

"Hold it, Lucio! It didn't help me that way. But something unimaginable happened one night."

"C'mon, Mario! Cut to the chase. What happened?"

"One of the prisoners asked permission to go and urinate. And from one end of the room where they kept us, the officers in charge shouted: "Hold on, and we'll take you." And so it happened. They walked up to him, told him to get up, and when he did, they led him along a kind of corridor that had formed between us, or rather, the sons of bitches pushed him along like guides for the blind towards a group of detainees. I was in that group."

"How did you know, if you were blindfolded?" asked Victor J., who still showed some scepticism, or at least he was the only one showing it openly.

"What happens is that your ear becomes keener to make up for the absence of sight. And I could hear them coming. "Stand up," they told him, and then came the order: "You can take a leak here." And I could feel him close by. "This guy doesn't know where he's going to urinate," I thought. "He probably thinks he has been taken out to the yard. They insisted: "C'mon, piss, we are not going to wait for you all day." There was a pause. "Did he pee in a corner?"

"No, wait. I could hear him unzipping his fly next to me and I thought: "These sons of bitches have brought him here, so he can pee all over me!" So I instinctively turned around and tried to hide my head like a boxer on the defensive, with my chin against my chest and my arms raised like levers to cover my ears."

Mario C. fixed his blue eyes on the audience. They were all mesmerised.

"C'mon, finish the story. Or else supper will be served and you will leave us in the dark."

"Wait, wait. The guy (I never knew who he was) lashed his urine all over me. He made me all wet: I could feel it on my back and my head, besides smelling the unmistakeable stench of urine. The smell labelled *sui generis* in biochemical tests. I called him all kinds of names. Poor guy, I was being unfair. He didn't even know where he was. Besides, I soon realised that I could get another beating for that."

"And what happened?"

"I could hear a distant voice telling me: Mario, don't complain. Human piss brings good luck. I shut up and chuckled. I could recognise that voice. It was my brother Juan Carlos's. That's the story."

Mario C. waited for an answer. It was an abrupt ending and something was missing, but he wanted to create suspense so his mates would ask him to go on.

"And what does that have to do with good luck?"

"Well, I'm here now. I have not been killed and I'm not a disappeared."

"And what about the others? What do you know about them?"

"They didn't get peed on, and they have been reported missing."

"How about your brother Juan Carlos?"

"I haven't heard his voice again. The old folks are still looking for him. You see? You have to get pissed on by a human being in order to be lucky."

No one uttered a word. Mario C. thought: "If only the guy peed on that night had been my brother!"

# The Dialectics of War

It was past supper-time and after each one of the prisoners had eaten in his cell and done the dishes, they all gathered around the central table in the ward. About fifteen of them were sitting, while the others were standing. They had come to an agreement about taking turns in the discussions, so that a certain order could be kept. Someone in charge made a mental note of the speakers and assigned them their turn following the order in which it had been requested. But these rules were never observed. The fact of the matter is they could not possibly be observed.

The prison authorities had forbidden meetings in the wards, at least since the coup of March 24, 1976. Living conditions had worsened, the food rations had been cut down, and family visits restricted, while cell inspections and corporal punishment had increased.

But in those days, at the end of December 1978, everything seemed to have taken a turn for the better: Wardens seemed kinder, and roast lamb had been restored on the menu; something new was in the air. The prolegomenon to a possible war with Chile had replaced a hellish life by a life of uncertainty.

The inmates were well-informed, not only through their relatives, but also through the wardens´ comments, and the clippings from the local newspapers rescued from censorship which tried to instill calm into the population and, at the same time, an eagerness for invasion.

Besides exchanging information, some resulting from wishful thinking rather than hard facts, the inmates discussed what would happen in the impending fight with Chilean troops, especially in the south, which was bound to become the stage for most of the battles to be fought.

They had heard sirens in the downtown area for the last few nights. When they asked the wardens what was going on, they answered bluntly and without euphemisms: "Blackouts and mock attacks at night."

"As far as I know, there have been blackouts not only in Rawson and Trelew, but also in Neuquén, Mendoza and San Juan. Apparently, even in Buenos Aires. Besides, my uncle, who is a civil pilot, has told the old folks they´re flying soldiers into Patagonia on commercial flights," Juan Carlos H. pointed out emphatically.

Then Ricardo V., regarded with distrust by some of the inmates because one of his brothers was an officer in the Navy, added, in a professorial tone, projecting his voice and taking advantage of his superior information sources: "Guys, everything has already been decided. The plan is called Operation *Soberanía*. The fleet will occupy some of the islands near the Magellan and Beagle straits. The Air

Force will then bomb Punta Arenas and Puerto Williams, and I have also been told that if necessary the Army will invade through the Puyehue pass in Neuquén, and from somewhere near Mendoza, as well as from the north. Videla even expects Peru's support, since it was defeated by Chile in the Pacific war."

Then he fell silent, as if considering the possibility of opening a period for questions and clarifications.

"Well, since you know so much, tell us what Pinochet intends to do," asked Victor V.

Ricardo V. willingly volunteered: "Well, don't forget the importance Chile attaches to its Patagonia. The Chilean government has fifteen thousand strong ready to be launched against the most important cities in the Argentine south, beginning with provincial capitals and other big cities: Ushuahia, Río Gallegos, Comodoro Rivadavia, Rawson and Neuquén, but not Viedma."

"Shit, Rawson! That's us," warned Demetrio L., adding what everybody knew and feared: "They may even drop bombs on the prison. After all, Pinochet knows he has no followers here."

That remark brought on laughter, partly because of Demetrio's original remark, and partly because of the inmates´ need to give vent to pent-up pressure. A generalised idea hovered above the prisoners about what could happen to them in the event of an attack. They knew the Argentine dictatorship hated them to death, and they also felt they were an enticing quarry for Pinochet, should he invade Argentina and make it to the south.

A siren went off nearby, the sign of a blackout. It was nearly eight o'clock. Suddenly, they could hear an alarm go off in the ward too. "Inmates, go back to your cells." The inmates obeyed, neither too fast, nor with the typical slowness that sometimes exasperates the wardens. They went into their cells pondering their immediate future, and the proximity and perhaps imminence of the war.

Very few were able to sleep that night, let alone the following nights. The end of the year drew closer and closer, and the news of a military build-up kept increasing: The Argentine war fleet was heading south, confirming Ricardo V.'s version. One of the headlines in the Trelew newspaper, which by then could be read uncensored, was a message from the Chilean Commander in Chief: "Get ready to start war right away. There may be attacks at any moment. Good luck."

The prisoners continued with their meetings, in an increasingly disorderly manner each time. The tension brought about by the uncertainty of what would happen to them mounted more and more. They had realised that although they could not change the course of external events, they should at least get ready for war.

Opinions were divided at that point, sharply divided. Some had favourable hopes in the case of armed conflict:

They thought they could attain freedom or generalised reductions in their sentences, or at least better conditions in everyday life, which, in actual fact, they had already been able to notice of late.

Carlos Z. was the utmost advocate of such points of view. As a matter of fact, Carlos Z. was an optimist by nature: He could always see the positive side to bad things. He had the attitude of a staunch believer who takes unfavourable circumstances as a test of his strength, only he was a layman. For example, he found an explanation for the reduction of days for family visits: "Maybe this is to save our families any suffering when they see us." And when they skimped that piece of fat beef, he would say that they were watching our cholesterol.

In the face of these belligerent circumstances, Carlos Z. and other inmates tried to find arguments in favour of war that would prove amenable to the prisoners. So one could occasionally hear: "Videla must plough all financial resources into the war, and he can save the expenditure we cause by freeing us or by allowing us to leave the country"; or else: "If they mobilise the armed and security forces for combat, they will need those in the penitentiary service we are withholding. You´ll see, they will end up going easier on the prisoners."

However, Indalesio J., a prisoner of communist extraction, expressed a view opposite to that of Carlos Z´s. Indalesio J. was always on his guard, like a boxer in the ring, ready for an artful blow or one below the belt. He was the kind of person who found a negative explanation for good circumstances. If we got better food he would say that they were trying to make us fat in order to sustain a transfer further south, or that they were going to take us to the Ushuahia penitentiary. If the ban on the newspapers and magazines left behind by visiting family members was slackened for a week, even if the real reason was the mere neglect or leniency of the wardens, he would argue: "Now they will demand that we recognise that the conditions in the prison are optimal. Whoever refuses will be screwed."

Besides, with regard to the almost inevitable air-raids, he would tirelessly repeat: "War can never favour the people, and if we are a part of the people, we do not have the right to expect that anything good will come of it."

Indalesio J., just like Carlos Z., was not alone in this. Several prisoners entertained the same views. If something unusual or novel took place in our prison lives, the consequences would be negative. They had no dearth of arguments for them, and the confirmation of facts almost always reinforced their fatalistic views.

When Christmas was drawing near, detention had reached fever pitch. It was on one of those days in the afternoon on the 20th or 21st of December that the prisoners in all of the wards could see several of the wardens walk along the halls in the company of ordinary prisoners carrying a big pot in one hand, and in the other a small one from which a paint roller was hanging, thus giving away what the pots contained.

They left the meeting and scrambled in front of their windows. They couldn't see them go up the stairs because these were internal. But they could see them on the roofs. The ordinary prisoners opened their pots. Then they dipped the rollers in, and as soon as they took them out, they rested them against the roof, which served as their floor and, bending over, they walked a few yards. This was repeated several times, as if they wanted to paint a strip. They always used white paint. After putting aside those pots, which made up the majority, they opened a few more. Then they applied coats of paint but differently this time, not in a horizontal manner. They were on the area they had previously painted white, but now they were writing letters or symbols. Everything lasted some three hours. Wardens and ordinary prisoners came back down. The inmates saw them walking along the halls, more relieved this time. The weight of the paint had stayed on the roof. They resumed their meeting. Naturally the question now was what had been written on the ward roofs facing the sky. It wasn't a matter of fixing leaks, since after all they had not painted the entire roof, but only the middle. The inmates, who fortunately did not have to put up with leaks on rainy days, had heard the heavy footfall on the roof.

Very few of them would later forget that Carlos C. said very confidently: "It's the same in every war: The civil targets, such as hospitals, schools and in this case the prison are marked with red crosses on a white background. Let us not forget that if there are air raids the Government has the obligation to communicate to its enemy in advance that we are not a military target."

Ricardo V. supported Carlos Z.'s point of view and, showing off his expertise, he lectured again: "We are witnessing the application of article fourteen of the Geneva Convention, to which both Argentina and Chile have subscribed. The parties will reach an agreement as to which areas and type of population will not be attacked. Undoubtedly we are one of those cases."

They all looked at Indalesio J., now expecting his approving nod at such an interpretation. It seemed reasonable and even reassuring.

It was then that Indalesio J., feeling everyone's gaze on him, folded his strong construction worker arms on his chest and said: "I agree with Carlos. Yes, they must have painted the roofs red and white." He paused, observing his mates' reaction: They stared at him utterly surprised that he agreed with Carlos Z. after all.

It must have been a few seconds, but that was all Indalesio J. needed to change his attitude, which had characterised him since he had come to prison.

He said: "True enough, they have painted a white background, but they must have written big red capital letters on the roof: BOMB HERE."

# Differential Treatment

In the Rawson penitentiary some inmates were constantly being picked on. Among those from the provinces, *cordobeses* and *tucumanos* bore most of the brunt; the former for having taken part directly or indirectly in the *Cordobazo*, or for being their genuine descendants; the latter for belonging to rural guerrilla bands, or for encouraging or simply showing some sympathy for the guerrilla movement.

The names that called for differential treatment were Juan Domingo, Vladimir, Fidel. Among the women, jailed in the Villa Devoto prison, those bearing the name of María Eva ran the same fate.

The social status of university professionals, whatever it might be, and that of plain workers, especially if rural, inescapably invited extra beatings.

The surnames with lots of consonants and few vowels of, in prison jargon, the *rusos*, the reds, attracted blows like an iron magnet. Prisoners of German, Polish, and Ukrainian descent suffered in their own flesh the worries of those who had difficulty pronouncing their names. Jewish prisoners were in for a bonus.

Haroldo T, a *Peronist* militant, knew this only too well. He had even witnessed some of this ill-treatment. However, he had not been a direct victim yet: He was neither *cordobés* nor *tucumano*, and his first and last names were not on the implicit list of hopeless cases. Being the descendant of Spanish parents, his last name was common and easy to pronounce. It is not that he had received preferential treatment, but he was one of them; until that day, the day of the interrogation by Intelligence Officers.

Some of the prisoners who had not been convicted, but were just under the surveillance of the PEN [National Executive Power], were subjected to periodical interrogations by penitentiary officers or officials from the Department of State.

After the usual reports, the national authorities would decide on a discretional basis whether to keep the detainees in prison, grant them full or supervised freedom, or else the right to leave the country, if they so chose.

Haroldo T. had received one of those "visits."

The order was barked out to him from behind the ward gate: "Inmate T., prepare to leave your cell!"

Later on, while Haroldo T. was going through the thick gate, not knowing why he was being summoned, they maliciously whispered in his ear: "The guys from the

Government are here to see how you are doing. If you give the right answers, you may perhaps be released."

"Those sons of bitches," grunted Haroldo T. to himself.

They led him along on a lead tied to the wrist of his right arm, forcing him to twist it round onto his back. "Dogs are put on a lead," he remembered.

The guardians had told him in advance the reason why he was being summoned. That enabled him to get ready. He should be careful when answering. He had few hopes of being released right away, but at least he didn't want to make things worse. "I mustn't confront them, he reflected."

The prison guard leading him tugged at the leash behind him, and shortly after he stopped at an office with its door closed. He knocked. Haroldo T. read the identifying sign: *Security Chief.* They could hear "Coming, just a moment" from the other side.

The moment stretched into several minutes. In the meantime, the guard tightened and loosened the leash on Haroldo T's wrist on and off, while he responded, as if in a blind game, by clenching and unclenching his fists to indicate he was being hurt. "I'm not going to tell him it hurts, or he will squeeze more tightly."

The door opened at last. "Let the inmate in. You can leave." The guard took the leash off his wrist, brought his heels together with a sharp clack from his boots, saluted the two interrogators martially, said to himself "Who the fuck do those guys think they are?" and, turning around, marched back to the ward.

"Come on in, inmate. Take a seat."

Haroldo T. sat on the chair they offered him, and rubbed his right wrist with the palm of his left hand to relieve the pain inflicted by the tightening leash. "Do you know why you've been brought here?"

"Yes, I was told on leaving the ward."

"Good, we're going to ask you a few questions. You can choose not to answer if you don't want to, and then the higher officers will decide what to do. Understand?"

"Perfectly all right."

The interrogators were not wearing a uniform. They both wore a grey suit; one wore a white shirt and the other a blue one. They both wore a tie and had short hair.

"We'll start with a few questions about yourself and your family. We could check your file, but we would rather you told us yourself, so we can get to know each other a bit. Agreed?"

"No problem," said Haroldo T., as he thought to himself: "These guys here want to soften me up. They think I'm an idiot."

"We'll then ask you about the jobs you´ve had, your political activism, and what you think about prison life. Of course you don't have to answer, but it's always advisable that you do, because that brings you closer to freedom, especially when you have a family."

"No problem."

"Let's start, then."

One of the interrogators opened a black briefcase, took out several forms, put in carbon paper between them, and got the sheets even by tapping them on the desk that separated him from Haroldo T. He raised his eyes.

"All right, first and last names?"

"Haroldo T."

"Birthplace and date of birth?"

Haroldo T. took a deep breath. He said to himself: "At least I'm not *cordobés* or *tucumano*."

"General Pico, La Pampa Province. December 18, 1948."

"Job?"

"Bank-clerk." Haroldo T. suppressed a smile: He was neither a professional nor a factory worker.

"If you are married, what is your wife's name?"

"Silvia A.."

"Can you remember her date of birth?"

"Yes." Haroldo T. remembered the surprises he had sprung on Silvia on several occasions, when, pretending to have forgotten her birthday, he would not give her a present until late in the evening. Small but warm: a book, half a dozen roses, a scarf.

He also remembered the joke one of the inmates, a mathematician, would often make: "Your birthday almost always is the same as your date of birth."

"January 15, 1950."

"Children?"

"Two."

"What's your first child´s name?"

Haroldo T. heaved another sigh. His children did not have any of the accursed names.

"Pedro Rafael."

"Rafael, after our president Videla?"

Haroldo T. didn't answer.

"I have asked you a question. Why don't you answer it?"

"My son was born in 1970. No one knew at the time our president would be Videla. No. My wife and I are very fond of the Renaissance Italian painter Rafael Sanzio. It was in his honour."

"Date of birth?"

"October 17, 1970."

One of the interrogators fidgeted uneasily. That date (the Peronist Workers Loyalty Day) had irritated him.

"Are you pulling our leg?"

"No, sir, why?"

"Because of the date, October 17. Do you think we are stupid?"

He remembered his mathematician prison mate again. And he repeated after him: "Every single day stands the same chance of being someone´s date of birth, one in three hundred and sixty-five, almost three in every thousand. My son just got that day."

"Come off it! Second child's name?"

"Cristina."

"Just one name?"

"Yes."

"Date of birth?"

Haroldo T. felt a cold sweat. "October 17, 19...," and a dead blow in his face left him speechless.

"Stand up, son of a bitch."

Haroldo T. got up from his chair as steadily as he could, and when he made to speak again, he got a punch in the stomach which made him double up, and left him breathless and speechless once again.

"You're getting smart on us, you motherfucker. You will rot away in here. So both your children were born on that same fucking day, eh?"

The two interrogators beat him tirelessly. They even took off their jackets to be more comfortable. Haroldo T., lying on the floor, bled by the nose and had a cut on his lower lip. He raised his right arm trying to get some attention.

That made the interrogators even more furious. One of them reproached him for not having apologised in time.

"What's wrong now? Are you going to apologise? It's too late, son of a bitch."

The other guy ventured an explanation for the coincidence in both his children´s date of birth: "You bastard, you waited for a few days, so the dates would coincide. These *Peronistas* are hopeless."

Finally, spitting blood and with a wan smile which was hard to understand given the circumstances, Haroldo T. said in a hardly audible voice: "No, what I´ve been attempting to say is that my children are twins, that's all."

# Science and Ideology

The prisoners were already in Rawson. All twelve of them had spent the night of August 22 in a small room, although each had been given his own mattress to sleep on. They were allowed to go to the lavatory every three hours, for which they had to get permission from the wardens. They were not too happy about the transfer, but it had not been so serious. Up until now.

It was seven in the morning by one of the watches that hadn't been confiscated, but still as dark as the night that had just gone by, as they could see through a small window high up.

"Come on, you bastards. Get up!!! Where do you think you are? All of you on your feet in a line."

All twelve of them got up in a hurry. The reception had just begun.

The Prison Security Chief, Alfredo G. -the inmate Víctor V. was to encounter him again twenty years later-, was harsh and fierce. Refined and cruel. He showed a rare desire to interrogate the detainees. He did so in such a way that the vertical relationship temporarily became an almost horizontal dialogue. Some prisoners took this as a sign of politeness or, even worse, understanding, but his true intention was to get to know their weaknesses, so he could then send in the rough wardens to soften them up.

The prisoners were handcuffed and, amid shouts, were taken to an interrogation room down a hall flanked by wardens who would hit them with their fists or truncheons. In that room intelligence officers tried, by means of threats, blows or promises, to wheedle out information that would serve different purposes: information that would be useful to identify and locate other "subversive" citizens, or else the detainees' weak points or their degree of dangerousness. On that basis they would then decide which ward each new prisoner should go to.

One by one the prisoners went from the room to a very small adjacent office. Handcuffed, they stood in front of three penitentiary officers and Alfredo G.. A resounding slap dealt when off-guard, that would rapidly make their cheek and ear go red and brought inevitable tears to the prisoners´ eyes, indicated that the interrogation had begun.

"Name?"

"Jorge H., sir."

"Where are you from?"

"Necochea, sir."

"Why have you been arrested, inmate?"

That was the first touchy question, accompanied by the permanent qualifying label he would get from now on. Alfredo G. and the officers knew full well why Jorge H. had been arrested. At least from the references they could read on the file sheets that would arrive with the transferred prisoners. They would wait for their answer and would study it.

Jorge H. vaguely knew the same as they did, but not exactly. "Because of my political activism in a part of Necochea," was his first pretence.

"Were you in the ERP [People's Revolutionary Army], inmate?"

"That's what I have been accused of, sir." That was a moderate, non-committal answer. It neither denied nor admitted the accusation.

"Don't play dumb, Jorgito. That´s what it says in your file."

"I have a clean record. I have been under the surveillance of the PEN for the last six months. That is what I'm being accused of, sir. But I have never been involved with ERP."

Alfredo G. addressed his subordinates: "Let him go to six. He then glared at Jorge H. and said: "I promise that if I find out you have lied to me, I will shut you up in the hole until you beg for your mother." That was Jorge H.'s first lesson: the hole must be a cell for punishment or confinement.

The twelve newly-arrived prisoners were questioned one by one. The last one to be interrogated was Pedro B., a Mathematics professor from the Universidad del Litoral. Actually, Pedro B. had never been an activist for any political party, although sensitive person that he was to injustice, he had taken part in public demonstrations and had signed petitions. He was an unprejudiced man, anti-dogmatic, and straightforward.

Alfredo G. was tired. The newly-arrived prisoners hadn't been very helpful. On this twenty-third of August his achievements had been very few so far. Besides, he had not been able to show off his histrionic skills in front of his subordinates, nor had he been successful at all in the interrogations. He would be the subject of gossip in the Officers´ Mess. He should do better than that.

"Inmate B., I read here that you are under the surveillance of the PEN on charges of trying to infiltrate Marxist ideology into the Universidad del Litoral. Is that true?"

"Yes, sir, but that's a mistake. I trust it will soon be cleared up and that I will be released."

"A mistake, eh? Who do you take me for?"

"No, sir, I taught Mathematics. I didn't teach anything related to politics or the ideology you mention."

Alfredo G. saw a glimmer of light in his uneventful day´s work: This was his chance to steer the interrogation to his own purposes by applying what he had learned in the courses on intelligence and counter-insurgency taken in Campo de Mayo.

"Tell me, inmate. Did you teach your students set theory?"

"Yes, sir. But if you allow me to say so, it is a generalised tool in secondary educational systems all over the world. We formalise it and teach it in greater depth at university level."

"Precisely that's the way Marxist infiltration works. It is first innocently inculcated in young people's impressionable minds."

Pedro B. made an effort not to lose his composure. If he answered he put his physical health at risk. Keeping quiet would be taken as an act of cowardice, which was quite unlike him: He would be casting a veil over the truth. "But sir, if you allow me, I can assure you that the creators of set theory lived long before Marxism came to be known as such. In fact, Cantor, a Russian mathematician who made one of the most important contributions to the field, died before Marx's work became widespread."

"Russian, you see. Proto-communist and proto-Marxist. And you, inmate, played up to them. You´ve been used like an idiot. That´s why you´re in prison."

"But sir, with all due respect, I can't see the connection. We could find so many Russian scientists or writers whose works preceded Marx who we couldn't possibly characterise as proto-communist or proto-Marxist, as you have done. With all due respect, sir."

"You use dialectics, inmate. How can you tell me you are not a Marxist?" The second slap could be heard. A slap given by a hand loaded with pain, humiliation, hierarchy and a peremptory command to mind one's words.

The assistant officers realised they should back up Alfredo G. One of them punched Pedro B. in the stomach, and when he bent over with pain, the other officer hit him across the back with his truncheon.

"Let me help you, inmate. Mention one of those hundreds of Russians you say did not pave the way for Communism. I challenge you to find at least one, and then I will let you go back to your ward." Alfredo G. was in his element. He felt like a winner.

Pedro B. searched his memory, still feeling the pain, compounded by the feeling of resignation before such a prejudiced man. This was the limit: He, an analytical person, having to make concessions. He couldn't decide which hurt more. He smiled. Suddenly he remembered the Tolstoy of *War and Peace.* "There is Leon Tolstoy, for example. In his novel *War and Peace* Napoleon, who had defeated the French, is depicted as the enemy." He heaved a sigh of relief.

Alfredo G. knew about the author too, so he took the bait to his advantage. "Ha! But Tolstoy also wrote Anna Karenina. And you, inmate, will surely remember that in that novel she falls in love out of wedlock. That's a big blow to one of the values most sacred to the Christian family. You see? You have no examples to give me, because you are like the whole lot of them."

He signalled to one of his assistants in order to enlist his support, and a clenched fist, which Pedro B. couldn't figure where it had come from, crashed into his stomach.

"Look, inmate. I'm going to give you one more chance. Give me one more name, or else admit that you are wrong and that you have indirectly promoted the Communist cause by teaching what you taught."

Alfredo G. felt triumphant again, not so much because of the blows that would generally soften the prisoners up, but because in his opinion Pedro B. didn't have any more arguments in this debate, and so he lowered his psychological guard.

Pedro B. felt sick, on the point of throwing up. Not so much because of the punches he had received, but because of his scorn for the dogmatic guy now facing him. He considered for a second apologising and giving up. Maybe that way there would be no more punches or bludgeons. They would send him to a ward for wimps, and not one for tough guys, which was a difference not to be sneered at. He felt like Galileo recanting in order to save his body from the stake, and saying in a low voice: "And yet it moves."

He shook his head as if rejecting this idea, which seemed conformist and forgiving to him. After all, unlike Galileo's, his life was not at risk this time.

He mustered up courage and addressing Alfredo G. said: "Sir, if you allow me, and with all due respect, before answering your question, I would like to know how old you are." Alfredo G. was taken aback, and asked in turn: "Why do you want to know?"

"Because I can tell you are a well-read and knowledgeable person, sir."

Alfredo G. could not possibly object to this, he even felt complimented by the prisoner's words and in a deep guttural voice replied: "Thank you. Forty-three."

Pedro B. stood as upright as he could and looked him in the eye, knowing in advance he would be showered with punches and blows, and aware of his future fate in that prison, proudly considered by prisoners and jailers alike as a maximum security prison. He cleared his throat: "How could a well-read man your age possibly be such a nitwit?"

# Sicilian Defence

Finally, everything was organised for the great challenge. The long-awaited chess game would now be played. Juan Carlos H. and Sebastián P. had signed up to compete, and their keenness to win foreshadowed a tough contest. They had both played chess in several Buenos Aires clubs and, judging by the rivals they had defeated and had been defeated by, they seemed even, which ensured a long and engaging nightly pastime for the spectators.

For an outside observer it would have been impossible to believe: games were forbidden in the Rawson Penitentiary, and you couldn't see boards or pieces in the cells.

Juan Carlos H. and Sebastián P. occupied adjacent cells almost in the middle of one of the ward wings, which allowed them, when they were both locked up, to communicate by means of taps on the wall, taking advantage of the absence of prison guards, especially at night. They had learned Morse code, so that they could hold conversations for the purposes of entertainment, or conveyance of some important information, such as transfers of detainees, unexpected visits, warnings of different kinds.

A tap given with the knuckle of the middle finger on the hard wall gave off a sharp sound, "tac" for normal ears, which stood for a point in the adopted code. Two consecutive taps without any pause between them, "tac-tac," meant a line. A small wait between the taps meant a change of letter or number, and a longer wait stood for a change in word. That was enough for each player to make his move known to his opponent.

Spectators would follow the development of the game by means of the same mechanism. Juan Carlos would reproduce the move made on the other side of the wall, while Sebastián would do the same on his side. That way the game could be easily followed, at least by a whole wing of the ward.

Only boards and pieces were needed in order to play and follow the game. That was not a problem either. Although they had no recreation materials at their disposal, they enjoyed two unequalled advantages: a wooden bed on which lay a mattress, and tea-bag envelopes with labels of different colours depending on the brand or function: for liver problems, diuretic, plain, and a hosts of others.

They would remove the mattresses and mark some of the wooden beams by scratching them with the bottom of toothpaste tubes. Thus they obtained a board with sixty-four squares, where thoughts would flow, and pieces made from those torn and folded labels would sail; pawns were distinguished from knights, bishops from castles, and black from white pieces.

Everything was now ready to begin. It had previously been agreed that Juan Carlos would get the white pieces, and therefore start the game. Once they had made sure there were no guards in the ward by checking under the door for the absence of penitentiary boots, it was announced that the game could safely begin. Rivals and spectators alike readied their artillery.

"Tac (pause), tac, tac, tac, tac, tac tac," was Juan Carlos H.´s gambit.

"Tac tac, tac, tac tac, tac (pause) tac, tac, tac, tac, tac," replied Sebastián P.

The two moves travelled through the walls that received the coded taps towards both ends of the ward, like the concentric waves produced when a pebble is thrown into a pond. A strange and simultaneous tension arose in the prisoners. For a moment Julio R. forgot that a few hours before he had received a letter from his wife where she told him about her intention, or rather, her decision, to separate, while asking for understanding and cooperation at the same time. It didn't matter to Benjamín S. either that his lawyer had informed him the day before that the National Executive Power (NEP), the government, the Presidency and its dependencies, the PEN, in prison jargon, had denied him the right to leave the country. His family would continue to be in Italy and he in Rawson.

The night was quiet, only punctuated by the taps on the wall: tac-tac. The game went on. Juan Carlos H. made his second move: "tac-tac, tac, tac-tac, tac (pause), tac, tac, tac-tac, tac (pause), tac, tac, tac, tac-tac, tac-tac."

Then came Sebastián P.´s response: "Tac (pause), tac tac, tac, tac, tac, tac."

The searchlights placed on top of the prison towers glided brightly across the empty yards, in which the guards hoped, perhaps, to find shadows of prisoners attempting a new escape. That light rhythmically stopped on the small window cells, making it possible for the prisoners to move their own pieces and so continue with the game.

It now shone on the third move. Juan Carlos H. announced: "tac-tac, tac, tac (pause), tac, tac, tac, tac-tac." Sebastián P.'s response followed: "tac, tac-tac, tac, tac- tac (pause), tac-tac, tac, tac, tac-tac (pause), tac, tac, tac, tac, tac-tac."

Jorge H., restless and itching to participate in the game, remarked in tap language from the back: "It's a Sicilian opening, it's going to be a tough game." It was impossible to reply to that; actually it was necessary to stop his interventions. Otherwise, the next moves would not be heard. All he got for an answer were dead blows on the wall not produced by knuckles, but by the side of the hand next to the little finger, which, made into a tight fist, demanded silence.

The game went on. An hour, one more hour, and then another went by unnoticed. For the prisoners, who found days to be as long as years, time flowed at an unusual speed, so they managed to stay awake and follow the moves. Only the tapping on the walls indicating a move or its reproduction broke the silence. Listen and tap, listen and tap.

Little by little the game took a course in favour of Juan Carlos H.: Even if they had exchanged queens and four pawns, his castles had found open columns, his bishops free diagonals, while his knights seemed willing to stay put for forever. Instead, Sebastián's castles were stuck on the first row as if in a siege. His bishops had only a few free squares around them, and the knights seemed unable to jump over the defence barrier patiently put around them by Juan Carlos H. It was a matter of a short time before checkmate and Sebastián P.´s acknowledgement of defeat. But he was not one to give up so easily. It wouldn't be a breeze for Juan Carlos H. No. He would first wait for a mistake on his opponent's part, a probability out of all proportion to the steadfastness and accuracy of his previous moves. Or perhaps an external cause or small miracle would paralyse the game.

That is exactly what Sebastián P. needed, a small miracle. Not an immediate release of all the prisoners that would provoke a generalised stampede in which everybody, Juan Carlos H. included, would forget the game being played. Not even the sudden announcement that they would exceptionally get an extra dinner, causing them to interrupt their supposed nocturnal rest.

Sebastián P. would have been happy with a lesser mishap, something that would require the cancellation or rather the abrupt interruption of the game, and would make it impossible to resume it. Only that could save him from a shameful defeat, and the subsequent mockery of his inmates.

Lying face down, his eyes riveted on the board, whilst he considered his predicament again and again, Juan Carlos H. now demanded an answer insistently: "So? So? (Tac-tac, tac, tac-tac, tac-tac)"-, and was about to tap on the wall to announce he was giving up, he and all the other inmates in the ward heard fist blows on the gate of one of the cells in the ward opposite, followed by a peremptory call: "Mr. Warden, Mr. Warden, please!."

"Who´s calling, and why? came the reply from the other side of the ward.

"It's inmate 235, in cell twenty-six. I urgently need to go to the lavatory."

"Use the pot, inmate. Do not make a disturbance at this time of night."

"I just *have* to go, Mr. Warden. Please open the gate."

"Just a moment, let me ask."

They all remained expectant. If the prisoner´s request was satisfied, at least two wardens would come in to escort the inmate to the lavatory, and turn on the cell lights for inspection. In that case they would have to hurriedly assemble the chessmen, put their mattresses back in place, tuck in sheets and blankets, lie down, and pretend to be asleep.

If the request was denied, the game would go on. This is what everybody wanted, except Sebastián P., naturally. Those minutes seemed like centuries, until finally the warden shouted from the gate: "Inmate in cell twenty-six. Get ready to go to the lavatory. Do you hear and understand me?"

"Yes, sir, thank you very much."

They could now hear the padlocks on the main gates being opened, and right after that two guards coming into the ward. They saw the lights go on from under the doors and realised that this chess game, with its Sicilian defence, was being abruptly brought to an end by a sudden emergency. Sebastián P. puffed with relief, raised his arms and eyes to a sky he could not see, and uttered, with an effort but with accuracy: "Thank you, Lord."

# The Good Guard

Pedro B. arrived at the ward he had been assigned. Because of his hostile attitude towards the Security Chief he got the first one, the ward assigned to *pesados* or dangerous criminals. He would soon get the chance to feel in his own flesh what that meant, not only because of the prison guards´ behaviour, but also because of that of his own prison mates. With his hands still behind his back holding with difficulty his few belongings (underwear, thick vests for the harsh Chubut winter, two or three pairs of socks and a few sweaters and shirts), he was brought to a halt at the front gate.

He remembered he was obliged to leave behind his trousers after the inspection on his arrival, for he was supposed to wear the official prison trousers, provided by the prison authorities. Neither could he bring his books with him. They were strictly forbidden.

With his eyes riveted on the floor, he heard the locks being opened and a voice saying "Open every other gate." He had already learned that this was a procedure to ensure only one gate was opened between two, so that the gate right behind should be locked. He was pushed into the ward.

"What's your name, inmate?"

"Pedro B., Mr. Guard."

"You can raise your head and look on both sides, so you get familiar with the place."

Pedro B. raised his head, politely wished him a good morning, and zealously turned his head right and left. It was a roofed rectangular building about forty yards long by twelve yards wide, with a large space in the middle with tables and long wooden benches. He thought he could see three or four gas heaters among the tables hissing loudly at the quiet surrounding area. Both the heaters and the silence struck him as odd. He was able to count twenty doors on either side. The cells, he thought.

The prison guard noticed his astonishment: "You know what, inmate? It's very cold in the winter and the heaters help. Your mates are locked up in their cells for security reasons, owing to your arrival. You will meet them soon. Would you like to take a shower?" he went on. "You will need it before we lock you up."

Pedro B. nodded "Yes sir, thank you very much. Where is the bathroom?"

"It´s on your left, behind the glass panels. It's a common area. Leave your clothes on one side. I´ll give you some soap and a towel."

Pedro B. headed towards the area the prison guard had pointed out to him. He took off all his clothes except his underwear. Despite the heaters near him he could feel the Rawson August cold just the same.

The guardian came within a yard or two near him. He stretched his hand and passed him a white towel and a bar of coarse soap. The kind used to wash clothes. The soap bar had that unmistakable smell of wax. It hadn't been used. It had sharp edges, just like wood that hasn't been sanded or smoothed out. He could read the brand name of the soap.

Pedro B. took off his underwear and could feel he was being watched by the guardian, who fixed his eyes on his naked humanity. It would be like this for years. While he was walking towards one of the showers Pedro B. thought: "It looks like there is at least one cool guy in here." He mechanically turned on the hot water all the way. No water came out. The guard sill watched him. Pedro B. insisted.

The guard opened a window in the glass panel. "Oh, sorry, I forgot, but there is no hot water. The boiler has broken down and spare parts are hard to come by in the area. We have already asked all inmates to be patient and to take cold showers in the meantime."

"Shit," muttered Pedro B, who was already shaking from his nudity, the low temperature and his fury.

"I beg your pardon, inmate?"

"Oh, nothing, sir. It's just a shame there's no hot water in this cold weather."

"Yes, indeed," added the guard, almost sympathetically.

Pedro B. plucked up courage, stood at arms´ length from the shower and turned on the cold water tap. The guard was still watching him.

He took a step forward, stood under the weak waterfall and felt his head and heart would burst. While the water was sliding down his body he soaped it as quickly as he could. He then put the bar of soap back on its dish, and walked away from the cold water in order to rub his head, pubis, testicles and butt. He must get rid of lice, fleas and ticks.

He got back under the water and swiftly rinsed out the soap. He took a step backwards one more time. He turned off the water. The guard was still watching him with indifferent eyes.

Pedro B. towelled his body steadily and expediently. When he was done, and had raised a foot to put on the underwear he was already holding in his hands, he heard the prison guard yet again:

"What are you doing, inmate?"

"Nothing, sir. I'm getting dressed. I have already showered. Thank you very much."

"Are you pulling my leg?"

"Not at all, sir. Why are you asking me?"

"There's still some soap left."

"Yes, sir. But I have soaped up my whole body. That is why I have dried and now I´m getting dressed."

"You will have to keep showering while there is still some of the soap I gave you. Don't get smart on me. And now go back to the shower. We want our prisoners very clean here."

# An Unpleasant Echo

Going to the dentist in the Rawson prison was undoubtedly painful. Those who visited him, always escorted by guards, complaining of toothache that prevented them from resting, thinking or even eating normally, knew that the answer was invariably the same: "Look, the only solution in your case is to have your tooth pulled out. I can give you my word for it." Sometimes it was a front tooth, sometimes a molar. You could even get multiple extractions. But the possibility of having a tooth fixed was out of the question "We don't have the right instruments or materials for that. You can take my word for it." The prisoners, feeling resigned while they prepared themselves mentally for the inevitable extraction, could imagine the dentist getting ready for the unpleasant procedure: First he put on his mask and latex gloves, and then put the chair lamp in the right position, which reminded them of the interrogations.

He directed the beam of light straight into the open mouth of the suffering patient.

"It'll only be a while. The pain will go away in a few days, and your life will soon go back to normal." He would grab the pincers right away and, stretching his arm, insert them in the mouth. His body followed the movement as if it were a human lever of sorts. It seemed as if he himself would get into the mouth of the poor prisoner, who looked both in awe and on the defensive.

Those who reacted quickly would stop that hawk-like motion over its prey. They would instinctively put up their arm, and sitting up would ask:

"Aren't you going to give me any anaesthetic?"

"There isn't any in the penitentiary. I don't know what´s happened, but it's been used up"

"And why didn't you tell me before? Do you intend to pull out my tooth just like that?"

"The thing is I'm just tired of insisting that they send anaesthetics and pain-relievers. You can take my word for it."

"They would be dumbstruck and finally surrender to the extraction. After all, the continuous pain that kept them sleepless and irritable was more unbearable than the temporary suffering inflicted by the pincers digging in their mouth and pulling out the tooth triumphantly.

"That's all right then, go ahead."

The pain you felt when you had a tooth wrenched out like that was beyond description. It wasn't even possible to close your eyes, because your mouth, which was wide open, so that it would not interfere with the drill or pincers, caused a superlative opening which involuntarily kept your eyes nailed to the ceiling.

When gripped by the instrument which started to move in a pendular fashion, so that it would loosen it from its base, the root took on a life of its own, as if it wished to be still welded to the bone that had given it support and a reason for being. But that effort was all in vain. Without anaesthetic, you could feel how the root, still trying to cling to the bone, was gradually pulled up. Suddenly, the entire piece was out, and with it came spasmodic pain while thick blood gushed out and was spat into the porcelain container. "You´re all set. It was a perfect extraction." The prisoners cursed that dentist again and again, promising revenge on this earth. The endless and unbearable pain caused by tooth decay had now vanished and replaced by this new pain which almost made them pass out, their eyes flushed by the tears it brought, and their throats gagging on the blood they had swallowed.

"Open your mouth, please. Let me put on some gauze so that it heals quickly. You'll have nothing to complain about in a few days. But mind you, no *mate* please. Because the suction may pull out the gauze plug; and don't smoke either to prevent nicotine from getting into the open wound"

The procedures were completed mechanically. Unable to speak, the prisoners would just nod their heads.

"All right, you can go now. As I say, you will have forgotten the pain in a couple of days. You can take my word for it. Do not thank me, it's my duty," he would always conclude.

The dentist was about thirty-five, colourless in every sense of the word. His uniform was grey and so was the way he treated the prisoners: his attitude was not one of commiseration or sympathy, nor was it offensive or impolite. He was just a bureaucrat doing his job, who accepted the conditions imposed on him without grousing. He would laconically say "I just obey orders." The prisoners eventually found out his name with the help of family and relatives: Jacinto O.

Gustavo P. had been one of his patients. He was a Psychology student at the Universidad de La Plata when he was arrested. And he had been in Rawson under the surveillance of the National Executive Power. "He's a PEN," was the expression used at the time to designate the thousands of detainees in the same plight.

With the decline of the dictatorship in 1982, he was set free. When he returned to his university the Psychology department had been closed down, so he enrolled in a different university and, while he busied himself doing home surveys, helping customers at a desk and offering new products, he gained a lot of experience dealing with people from all walks of life, which, coupled with his professional expertise, swiftly turned him into a respectable Human Resources Manager.

In 2002, with the boom of the oil industry in a revived and prospering Comodoro Rivadavia, most of the companies decided to expand and hire more personnel. That is why *Petroleum Argentina*, anticipating the employment of over a hundred workers, was on the look-out for a resident dentist, among other health professionals, who would tend to the new workers and the rest of the staff.

The head of Human Resources advertised a position in the local papers: "PETROLEUM ARGENTINA SEEKING FULL-TIME DENTIST. PLEASE VISIT OUR OFFICES ON MOSCONI AVENUE 1230. FROM 10 AM. TO 1 PM. HUMAN RESOURCES. KINDLY SEND CV BY ELECTRONIC MAIL TO recursoshumanos@petsur.com.ar."

Jacinto O. was one of the candidates to send in his CV. He had already moved to the largest city in Chubut. Life had become tough with the advent of democracy. The Chubut College of Dentists had revoked his membership for violations of the professional ethics code, his wife had succumbed to a severe clinical depression, and his two children had distanced themselves from him both physically and emotionally on finding out the reasons for their father's dismissal from the professional association. And he was banned from working for any health care provider or in any public hospital, as his licence had been revoked for 99 years.

Besides, he was already sixty. At that age, depending on the occasional private patients who would walk into his office proved terribly painful.

He arrived punctually for the interview. But he was not the first one. There were two other candidates ahead of him. It was finally his turn. He was ushered into a large office where a man who must have been around fifty was waiting behind a sober-looking desk. Behind the host's back, one could see the Argentine sea through a large window. It was rough, as usual.

The manager stood up and kindly put out his right hand. "Good morning. Are you Jacinto O.?" Without waiting for a response, he added: "Please, take a seat. I have read your resumé."

It seemed to Gustavo P. that he was in front of a vaguely familiar face. But he dismissed this as irrelevant.

"As you know, we're looking for an experienced dentist, and your CV looks quite impressive."

"Thank you!."

"However, I have noticed an inconsistency. You indicate in your CV that you have worked in the public sector for almost twenty-five years, but eight years in the Posadas Hospital and nine in the Municipal Hospital in Bahía Blanca only comes to seventeen years."

"Actually, I worked for almost ten years, between 1975 and 1984, for the Federal Penitentiary Service."

Gustavo P. gulped, trying to conceal his anxiety: "Where exactly?"

"In the Rawson Penitentiary. But whenever I mention it or include it in my CV, I'm in trouble." Then he added, almost with a sigh: "The fact is things have changed so much now."

Gustavo P. was still astonished: "I don't know what to do," he thought to himself. "I'm paralysed, I have sworn to seek and take revenge on all the guys that made me suffer so much. I have tried to keep alive in my memory their names, faces and gestures, so as not to forget them. I have tried to find out the addresses of all those who brought so much pain upon us, in order to take revenge, but now that one of them is right here in front of me, I can only take pity on him. He has really caught me off guard."

He barely managed to say: "Well, I understand now. Don't worry. We will give your CV all the attention it deserves. You have very rich experience, no doubt gained in difficult circumstances, in which I'm sure you didn't even have enough equipment to work properly. I guess you must have had a hard time trying to treat your patients and prevent them from suffering, making sure their pain would not be aggravated in their harsh imprisonment."

"I just did what I could. That's all."

"Don't worry. As I was saying, we will carefully consider your application. You will hear from us shortly." Then he added: "You *do* have some chance," trying to raise the candidate´s hopes. These last few words from Gustavo P. caused Jacinto O.'s cold and distant look to brighten up. "I'll be forever grateful for whatever you can do. Actually, I´m in dire need of that job."

Gustavo P. stood up gesturing to Jacinto O. to follow suit, and then walked him to the door.

He shook hands with him, emphasising one more time that he would consider his application seriously, and in order to ratify his commitment he found the exact words, the ones he had been wanting to utter since he realised who it was he was interviewing. Ceremoniously, trying to give him reassurance and hope, he said: "You can take my word for it."

# Dreams of Freedom

Juan H. and Bernardo A. were ready to leave. It was about four in the afternoon. They were able to calculate the time because the *mate cocido* had already been served in the ward. And that was the time when they brought in the sweating and boiling pot which gave off an unmistakeable smell, transformed into an exquisite scent by the prisoners´ permanent state of hunger.

In the morning they had been summoned to the gate and curtly addressed: "Inmates H. and A., get your personal belongings ready. You will leave this ward this afternoon." At least now they were told in advance. The worst times, with their sudden and rough shifts at night, and uncertain destinations, had now declined, even if they hadn't disappeared altogether. Besides, that July in 1980 seemed somewhat favourable: A good batch of non-convicts had been set free or, after much deliberation, had been granted the right to leave the country.

Juan H. and Bernardo A., besides being ward mates, had also been political militants together. They were both members of the People's Revolutionary Army, the "prabies" in prison jargon. They were from Córdoba. Moreover, they had never had the chance of a fair trial, and having been arrested at the beginning of April of 1976, they were now under the surveillance of the Executive, on account of the state of siege.

Juan H. and Bernardo A. went to their cells, and wrapped their belongings up in a blanket, which they had previously stretched out on the rough bed. After taking their few possessions off the shelves −boxer shorts, vests, shirts, socks, a pair of tennis shoes, letters and photographs-, they took the four corners of the blanket and knotted it into a bundle. They left the *yerba*, sugar and biscuits for the other prisoners, but no cigarettes. They were ready. Their prison mates did not take long to stop by and say goodbye, despite the prohibitions. Both Juan H. and Bernardo A. received both the warmth and queries from those left behind.

"Do you know where you're going yet? Are you being transferred? Or are you being released?"

"Watch out! Does your family know? Don´t let them screw you."

"I envy you, son of a gun. If you're really going back home, I wish you good luck."

"Have you been given the option of leaving the country? You asked for Spain, didn't you?"

Juan H. and Bernardo A. were uneasy and confused. They were uncertain about their near future and the fate of their lives.

After the farewells they started exchanging questions. "Why should we be released at the same time? Are we both being set free? Maybe we are just being relocated." Suddenly, the officer on duty came up to the main gate, and called out in a low-pitched, projected voice: "Inmates H. and A., report at once!"

Juan H. and Bernardo A. hastened to the gate. They put their hands behind their backs and stood in front of the officer, one next to the other.

"You've been told that you are leaving this ward, haven't you?"

"Yes, sir."

"Do you know where you're going?"

"No, sir."

"Let me tell you then."

All the inmates fell silent and turned their face towards the front gate, trying to hear, straight from the horse's mouth, where H. and A. were being sent.

"One of you is being released. The other will be transferred. For security reasons, I'm not allowed to tell you which of you will be set free or the other's destination. I'm sorry. I hope you understand. Good afternoon."

Juan H. and Bernardo A. were dumbstruck. The entire ward was in total silence, so that one could only hear the hissing burners consuming gas.

"Didn´t you hear I said 'good afternoon'?"

With a lump in their throat they both answered: "Good afternoon, sir."

A sadist couldn't have done it better. They would rather not know at all than to half-know. Each one privately hoped to be the one being released, but he immediately felt ashamed, because that meant prolonging his mate's imprisonment. Each had enough reason to believe he would be definitely freed and not merely transferred.

They mustered enough courage to discuss it between them. Juan H. said: "I'm sure it's you. They surely know that I had a more important position and higher responsibility in the *Orga* [armed organisation]."

"Do you think so?" Asked Bernardo A. with mixed feelings wavering between the desire that Juan H.'s reasonable argumentation was shared by those who had made the decision, and an awareness of his human misery for entertaining that thought.

"Sure. Don't forget that I've been punished several times. Here, in Rawson, and in Villa Devoto."

"Yes, but only God knows if that´s enough." Deep down, however, he wished that mere fact was enough.

"Besides, your family has tried to get you out. I am alone in this world, Bernardo."

"Let's wait awhile, until evening, and you'll see I'm right. Besides, your being freed is as if I was being freed a little too."

Tears welled up in Juan H.,'s eyes. He smiled and, by way of an apology, even if he had nothing to apologise for, said: "Oh, I must be getting old, I guess."

Bernardo A. realised he had never had, and probably would never have, that unique spirit of solidarity and that selflessness that, like now, Juan H. often showed.

He gave him a tight hug. The other inmates, who had kept at a distance from Juan H. and Bernardo A, aware that they needed to be by themselves, now gradually approached and tried to comfort them.

"Well, at least one of you is leaving, and the other one will have a change of air."

"The onc being freed will help the one staying behind."

Actually, Juan H. did not feel any sorrow. He believed, rather, he was sure, that his mate Bernardo A. would be released, and not at his expense. The logic was irrefutable.

"Move around, inmates, move around."

A scarce half hour later, the call was heard from the gate: "Inmates H. and A., report for exit with your belongings. No farewells."

Juan H. and Bernardo A. quickly walked into their cells and came out with their light loads. One of them remembered the words of Joan Manuel Serrat's song: "Travel light." He smiled.

They stood before the gate and the liturgy began: "All inmates must stand back, two inmates are leaving."

Bernardo A. did not feel guilty, but instead grateful to those inmates he would leave behind in a few seconds, never to see them again, at least not in prison. Suddenly, while the warden was sticking the key in the lock and turning it, he turned around, put his bundle of things on the ground, and raising his left arm in a fist, screamed at the top of his lungs. He screamed for all he had left unsaid, for all he had suffered, and for all he was leaving behind: "Comrades, we shall overcome!"

"Come here, you idiot!" The guards, with the gate now open, grabbed him by the arm twisting it behind his back and hit him on the head with tight fists. "You fucking idiot, who the fuck do you think you are? Che Guevara?" But he didn't care, it was a small price compared to all the suffering he had had to endure. Besides, these would be the last blows. They led them away together, one next to the other, in complete silence. They were stopped at the end of the hall. "It's two of them: a release and a transfer." This was the parting of the ways.

Juan H. just said: "Good luck outside." Suddenly, against their expectations, they heard the officer on duty, the same guy who had told them about their destinations earlier on: "Good luck outside? What are you talking about? You are the one being released."

"Me?"

"Yes, right now." And addressing Bernardo A., who had turned pale, he added: "You are being transferred." He relished each word, anticipating with pleasure the hurt the words would cause. "You're going to ward six, but before that you will spend ten days in the hole. Next time you will think twice before getting smart on us, you pinko!"

# Twelve or Thirteen

There were thirteen of them. They knew it. They had been made to number themselves at least three times. Now they were seated with their few belongings in an old refashioned plane waiting to start their trip from Bahía Blanca to Trelew, and from there to the Rawson Penitentiary.

Some had been sentenced by a federal court, others by martial courts, others had been under the surveillance of the Executive for quite some time, not knowing how much longer that situation would last, while others had been taken from an underground detention camp. These were in a pitiful state. Thirteen, there were thirteen of them, that damned unlucky number, remembered Carlos H. as he watched the afternoon sun setting on the bay.

They were not blindfolded, but they were handcuffed. Paradoxically, following international regulations, their seat-belts had been fastened. At the head of the runway, the pilot revved up the engine. The federal penitentiary service staff in charge of the prisoners took their seats too and fastened their seat-belts. After taxing briefly, much more briefly than heavy commercial aircraft, the plane took off.

As he looked through the window at the sea inlet in Puerto Ingeniero White, Juan C. remembered his last family visit in the Villa Floresta prison: "It was quite enjoyable. I held my children in my arms. They are so big now! My wife looked sad. I don´t blame her. But I could at least see them once a week. Now, when the fuck will I get to see them again?"

Pedro H. also complained about the transfer: from being librarian in the common Villa Floresta prison he would end up in a maximum security prison! "Little Pedro, get ready for hard times," he told himself.

As a matter of fact, deep down they all complained about the change in destination, except those who had arrived at the airport in a worse state on account of the torture and hunger they had been subjected to. They knew things would be harsher. No more visits, books, magazines, newspapers, or the radio. Nothing at all. The Rawson prison was notorious for its severe discipline and isolation. To make matters worse, they would arrive on August 22, the fifth anniversary of the prison break-out and slaughter at Zar air base. It couldn´t have been a worse date for arrival.

When the plane reached cruising altitude the penitentiary officers started to walk up and down the aisle, making sure seatbelts were still fastened and that handcuffs were still tight on their wrists. "The game is up, you sons of bitches," said one of the officers, who then added: "Those who make it to the penitentiary will now get to know what a real prison is really like."

"Those who make it? Why those who make it?" Gabriel H. asked himself.

"My family knew of the transfer, they had even been informed of the date, and I signed out myself" Alberto R. reminded himself, trying to stay calm.

At the back of the plane, Juan L. wondered whether the threatening expression had been addressed to him; after all, he had been taken with a hood over his head and face from the place where he´d been kidnapped to the plane staircase. Besides, he was from Trelew. "Perhaps they mean to interrogate me there," he thought, and his body was seized by a light yet steady trembling, which he was unable to shake off, despite all his efforts.

After a while, the plane started its descent. The detainees sat upright, buckled up their seatbelts and the plane touched down shortly after. The prisoners noticed vehicles and armed officers deployed beside the aircraft. There was no more daylight. The spotlights were on, and a beam shone down from the control tower, like a lighthouse. They could see a patrol wagon, two vans and twelve men in uniform.

The prisoners were quickly led down the staircase while the penitentiary agents at the bottom who were in charge of their reception counted them: one, two, three, four ... thirteen of them in all.

"Everything is fine," roared the young penitentiary officer in charge of the air transfer. The pride he felt at having carried out his mission successfully caused his chest to swell.

"Good," the officer receiving the detainees answered laconically. He was middle-aged, with salt and pepper hair, and about to retire, taking advantage of the virtues of a working arrangement in which each year counted double if you worked in an area with a harsh climate, like Patagonia.

"Please sign this reception form. And here´s the roster with the names and particulars of all the detainees being transferred to the Rawson penitentiary unit. The roster also contains a brief description of their legal situation. They should be sent to the building you judge appropriate, depending on how dangerous they are. Their record files should be arriving in a few days.

"Fine," said the major, somewhat uneasy at the martial and peremptory tone of someone who was addressing him as if he were his superior, even if he had a lower rank. "This upstart feels confident because he has the advantage of working for those who don´t abide by the law," he thought. "I don´t approve of subversion, but these guys should not be treated like animals either."

After reading out their names, he realised there was one prisoner missing. "I can see twelve names with their particulars here on the list, but thirteen have got off the plane and been handed over to me to be taken to the penitentiary," he observed.

"That´s right. One of the prisoners will be taken away from the penitentiary unit by military personnel early tomorrow morning."

"That´s as good as saying that I must keep one of the detainees for one night off the record."

"That´s correct."

"But that´s against all regulations!"

"Those were the orders, sir." Please sign here. I ought to fly back to Bahía Blanca as soon as possible. Besides, we have a few more transfers this week."

The officer looked at the subordinates that had come with him. They were standing close behind him, one on his right and one on his left. His eyes showed the rage he couldn´t express in words. He bit the bullet and signed.

"Thank you so much, sir. Good night."

"Good night."

By now, the thirteen prisoners were in the patrol wagon. With their few belongings in a bundle, each one of them stood in a reduced space like a tube, under one square metre and 1.80 metres high. They were still handcuffed.

"Begin," ordered the older officer, and the wagon and the other vehicles drove off. He and his assistant officers rode in the first car, followed by three agents in the patrol wagon, and finally a van with six more agents.

"There´s twelve of us, and thirteen of them, not twelve," thought the major with a smile on his face. One of his subordinates was driving the car, and the other sat right behind him. He trusted them. He´d known them for over fifteen years. They had often had to team up together, as in Rawson now. None of them approved of the military government in power, but they had not had the courage to voice their dissent, or to quietly resign. Somehow or other they had found justification in the fact that they had a family to support, knowing full well it was a cowardly and false excuse.

"Shit!," exclaimed the officer, and abruptly asked his subordinates: "Do you know what´s going to happen? One of those young men will be disappeared tomorrow, and we will be accomplices!." The assistants agreed, both the driver, intent on staying on the thin thread of paved road leading into the shadows, and the man in the back seat, now remembering his father, who had also been a penitentiary agent just like him, now retired, and who had warned him early on: "My son, think it over before entering the service. One day you will be obliged to do something that will make you less of a man. I was obliged to do so and you will be too."

They were approaching Rawson.

The officer ordered the driver to slow down and pull over. The patrol wagon stopped too, as did the van in the rear.

"Come on!" shouted the older officer as he got out of the car and headed for the back door of the patrol wagon.

"Something wrong, sir?" asked the driver after winding down the window.

"Not at all. Just the opposite. Please open the door and let the prisoners out."

His order was carried out. The prisoners got out one by one, fearing the worst.

"Gentlemen. I will read out the roster. When I call your name, you should take a step forward.

"Jorge A.?" "Here!"

"Esteban C.?" "Here!"

"Carlos H.?" "Here!"

"Alberto M.?" "Here!"

The prisoners trembled with fear. All twelve names were read out, except Juan L.´s. He was the thirteenth man, the man not on the list, whose fate was uncertain.

"What´s your name?"

"Juan L."

He took him by the arm and drew him apart a few yards. "Look here, L. There must be a mistake. Your name is not on the list, so I can´t take you to the penitentiary. Instead, what I´ll do is take you to the provincial court and inform the judge. He has a good reputation, you see, so he doesn´t like any shady stuff. I will let the bishop know too, and will ask him to go to the court right away.

"Thank you, sir!"

"Not at all!"

"Get back in," ordered the major. We will stop at the court on our way to the prison. We need to drop a transferred prisoner off who hasn´t been identified. Then I´ll make a couple of phone calls and will be on our way to unit 9."

The convoy set off again. They stopped at the court, the major exchanged a few words with the officials on duty and asked the unidentified detainee to get out of the wagon. After that, the major dialled a phone number and the bishop woke up with a start: He hung up, hastily got dressed and went out into the cold night of August 22. Meanwhile, the judge told his alarmed wife that he was going to the court, where a handcuffed detainee by the name of Juan L. had been left.

Finally the three vehicles reached the penitentiary and pulled up at the check-point, where the officers on duty asked for ID, following procedure, which the major duly produced.

The officers on duty saluted and, more relaxed now, asked if there was any news.

"Twelve inmates are entering the penitentiary. Take the roster, please. They are all in the wagon. Have them taken to the Infirmary for a check-up and their health condition noted down. Please check all the transferred prisoners´ identity. I don´t want any unpleasant surprises, since I´ll be taking a long vacation as of tomorrow."

# The Confession

Monday afternoon.

"Look, several of the inmates have already done it. Of course you are under no obligation, but there is no doubt that if you write and sign a statement admitting the mistakes you made, you will have more chance of having your sentence revised or commuted."

"What do you mean, admitting the mistakes I made?"

"Well, just indicate that times have changed, that you have changed, that the methods you used in order to attain power were not the right ones, that you swear to abjure arms, and that you intend to get back into democratic life. All that. I'm leaving ten blank sheets of paper and a pen. You know that for security reasons this is not allowed, but this case calls for an exception. When you´re done, please return all the sheets, the ones you have written on as well as the ones you haven´t used. Think it over, please."

"Yes, I'm going to think about it."

"Well, but keep in mind that we will be collecting all the letters from the penitentiary in twenty-four hours. Today is Monday, so you should return the signed statement by tomorrow afternoon. Anyway, I'm at your disposal, should you have any questions or concerns. We firmly believe you can be reclaimed for society. That means we could undertake to file for a reduction of your sentence. Have a good day."

"Have a good day."

Juan Carlos H. knew it. Towards 1978 and shortly before the Soccer World Cup, the military government had randomly picked a few prisoners from all over the country expecting that they would sign a document in which they stated their ideological change and acknowledged their mistakes.

It had never crossed his mind he would be one of the chosen. He had first been taken to the Governor's Office to be informed beforehand that he would be visited by an official from the State Department. He had also been informed about the reasons for this visit, and had been encouraged to agree to this compromise. Besides, they would go to his own cell, so that he could feel safe.

Juan Carlos H. remembered and smiled when he repeated the words that had been said to him at that moment: "Besides, you will feel more at ease that way, though of course it won´t be like being at home." "It's not my home. Of course it's not," he answered.

He had been serving a long twelve-year sentence determined by the federal judge in Santa Fé. Juan Carlos H. had been a railroad union leader, very popular among his co-workers, and as a result of all the strikes to stop the closing of railroads and repair yards, the military dictatorship had first abducted him and then sent him to trial, charged with destroying railroads, disobeying the authorities, agitating the workers and carrying weapons of war on him. He was 33 years old now.

But the worst was not yet over. The worst thing imaginable was happening right now. All the tortures he had been subjected to were now behind him. Even Rawson prison with its severe rules did not turn out to be insurmountable. The worst part of all was being separated from his family. His children, Daniela and Juan Domingo, would now be in school, he reckoned. For the last three months he had not heard from his wife, Susana, who had never really understood or approved of his activism. He didn't know whether she had written to him and the letters had been intercepted, or whether she preferred to add more distance between them. His mother had visited him the month before and, although she had told him about his children, she had avoided talking about Susana altogether.

And now this! Other prisoners had already warned him: They will come and put pressure on you. The military are trying to improve their international image. They want to show that the prisoners have admitted, after careful reflection, the mistakes they have made, and they intend to resume their normal lives in society democratically and honouring the Constitution.

Juan Carlos H. had answered: "But what democracy and Constitution are they talking about? They have violated democratic laws and have sent the Constitution to a better life. When they came to power, they even swore by a statute of the National Reorganisation Process, not by the Constitution."

And Juan Carlos H. was an ideal prey to show his willingness to be reformed. He had been a railroad worker since he was eighteen, very cooperative and well-liked by his mates. He had even won the elections of the railroad union. His most daring, or maybe noblest, co-workers would visit his mother to give her reports on their jobs and their difficulties, and would also pass on his love and affection.

When the official left his cell, he remained sitting thoughtfully on his bunk. That is how he was found by his two best ward mates: Hector Z., a History teacher who had introduced him to the study of the labour struggle in Argentina, and Aníbal P., a worker in the sugar refineries in Tucumán. They were very different: while the first was serious-looking and reserved, the second was chirpy and outgoing.

Aníbal P. drew a vertical movement upward with his head, as if questioning Juan Carlos H. To make sure, he asked: "Was it the guy from the government?" And without waiting for a reply, he added "What did they offer you in return?"

Héctor Z., who addressed no one with the familiar you, or thou, (*vos*), did not wait for an answer: "Well, don't worry too much. The decision is ultimately yours."

"Yes, it is *my* decision. But what the fuck should I do?"

"You could write a statement without committing yourself too much," said Aníbal P. encouragingly.

"You think about it, Juan Carlos. You are a man of principles. Besides, the dictatorship will come to an end sometime, hopefully soon. Moreover we can't be too sure whether they will keep their promise," said Héctor Z.

They kept on exchanging opinions for a while. In the process Juan Carlos H. found out that several of the inmates in the prison had already submitted their repentance statements, in other prisons as well. And those who had been convicted without a trial were given the option of leaving the country.

They had supper. Shortly after, each one of the prisoners went back to his cell to rest. But Juan Carlos H. could get no rest. He kept thinking all night, sitting on his bunk bed, holding his head between those rough hands of his, his elbows sinking into the concrete table. He wavered between agreeing to the compromise being proposed by the Government (which, like a cunning mermaid, lured him into starting anew in life) and flatly rejecting it, thus making even more improbable his chances of going back to his loved ones and his co-workers.

Tuesday morning.

After breakfast, Juan Carlos H. went back to his cell. He requested permission not to go out into the playground. Instead, he preferred to stay alone and sacrifice the only precious hour during which he could walk freely at leisure.

When his ward mates went out to enjoy that benefit in the open, Juan Carlos H. saw the Security Chief enter his cell. This was unusual. Everything had seemed unusual to Juan Carlos H. since the previous Monday.

When he had been tortured, he knew he had to hold out for as long as he could. And he did so. When he was sentenced, he tried to appear strong, so that his family would suffer less; and during his imprisonment he had never shown any weakness, nor had he ever cringed. But this was different.

"It looks like you are leaving us, inmate."

"I don't think so, sir. Everything is so confusing."

"Remember that the Government has a lot of hope in you. We think you can be reclaimed for society."

"Just by signing a repentance statement? That sounds weird."

"What I know is that those statements will be gradually published in the media, especially in those places where the prisoners come from. And that is quite a commitment."

"Oh, yes."

"Do you have a piece of paper and a pen, inmate?"

"Yes, sir. They supplied me with plenty of paper yesterday. Look, I have ten sheets. Apparently there is a lot I have to repent of," said Juan Carlos H. tentatively.

"That's a good joke. Don't exaggerate. I will leave you by yourself now, but I strongly advise you to take advantage of this unique opportunity. See you later, inmate."

"See you later, sir."

Héctor Z. and Aníbal P. returned from outside and stood in front of Juan Carlos H., who was sitting in the same position as they had left him, except that now he had a few sheets of paper on his table, and on them a blue pen with its cap on the side.

They chose not to ask any questions. Noon came and the prisoners went with their trays to get their meal. Juan Carlos H. couldn't swallow a bite. He could barely drink water.

Tuesday was mail day. Juan Carlos H. needed a letter from his wife, even if he wasn't expecting it. He was wrong. "Inmate Juan Carlos H., there is a letter for you," someone called out from the gate.

He walked up to the gate with a mixture of fear and anticipation. He took the envelope, which had already been slit open. He took out the letter and noticed that his hand was shaking. He started to read.

Susana told him about their children's progress in school, where they seemed to be doing well. She also told him about other family members, with that effort and style characteristically used by prisoners and their families in order to communicate certain information, despite censorship.

Then he read a disquieting paragraph in which Susana told him that officials from the State Department had come to see her, and that depending on what he did, he would perhaps be released before his time was out. That is why she asked him to make an effort and to think about his family. He felt he was choking.

That was not all. In another paragraph, which he read as a veiled threat, she pointed out this would be an important test for the value he attached to his children and wife, and that her future actions depended heavily on what he finally decided.

He walked back to his cell, his vision blurred, and sat, or rather let himself fall on, the rough bed. His face was noticeably pale.

A few minutes went by and the cell doors were closed, so that the prisoners could get their afternoon rest. Once the rest period was over, Héctor Z. and Aníbal P. came to talk to Juan Carlos H. But he stopped them kindly but firmly: "I would rather be by myself, sorry." The paper was still on the table, but they couldn't get to see whether Juan Carlos H. had written anything.

At five o'clock the prisoners were instructed to head back to their cells, and the ward gates were opened. A man in a suit walked up to Juan Carlos H.'s cell. It was the same man who had made the proposal the day before. "Good afternoon, H.," he greeted.

The prisoner stood up, taken aback.

"Good afternoon, sir."

"Have you made up your mind?"

"Yes, sir"

"May I have those sheets back then?"

"Of course." Suddenly Juan Carlos H. summoned as much courage as he could from he didn't know where, took the sheets, and stacked them carefully.

And making wet the thumb and forefinger of his right hand, he handed back the sheets one by one as he counted: "one, two, three, four, five, six, seven, eight, nine and ten," as if he was just beginning to learn to read and write. The sheets were all blank. When he finished counting he added: "You know, I'm just a railroad worker. I barely completed my elementary education, and I find it very hard to write."

# Politeness Rules

They all fell silent. They fell silent and turned their heads towards the main gate of ward six, where the prison warden, beside himself with rage, on the edge of a nervous breakdown, shouted behind the bars: "What else, inmate? What else?!!!," waiting for the right answer from his addressee, and expecting him to act accordingly.

The inmate in question was Esteban T., notorious for his involuntary affronts, stemming from a rare combination of lack of memory and knowledge (or rejection) of the expected social rules and conventions. The legend went around among the prisoners that Esteban T. had parked his car with his small children inside, and had gone to do the shopping in a supermarket leaving them abandoned for hours; and that he rarely tied his shoelaces, or that it was not uncommon to find him walking in odd shoes. In addition, the dates he had stood up were countless.

The point was that protocol dictated that whenever a prisoner addressed a warden verbally, he should always use "mister". This form of address conferred upon the wardens a status as high as the severe decrease in self-esteem experienced by those who had to inevitably appeal to such formulae in order to obtain not only what they needed, but sometimes a mere answer.

But this is what the Rawson penitentiary was like, and it couldn´t be helped. It was the winter of 1978, and maximum security measures made themselves felt. Family visits were forbidden, as was any physical contact with the detainees. The prisoners' children grew bigger, while their fathers grew older on the other side of the glass panel through which they saw one another. Communication took place through a pipe from which two horns emerged, one on either side, while the rest was kept hidden, making them wonder whether the verbal messages were recorded or not.

Physical activity, including sports or just jogging, were banned too, so that the prisoners were only allowed daily one-hour walks in the playground. During that time, taking advantage of the absence of the prisoners, the penitentiary personnel conducted searches in the cells, confiscating whatever they considered to be dangerous. They utilised a classification system so arbitrary, that what was dangerous one day was not the next. It could be matches, jam jars, paper or letters from family.

Meanwhile the Federal Judge in Rawson declared the prison to be one more front of the war against subversion, so that he would rarely consider complaints of prison abuse, or if he did, they never succeeded. Such behaviour was perfectly matched by that of the chaplain of the penitentiary unit, U9 in prison jargon, who on each visit would recommend with a pat on the cheek which sounded more like a slap: "Dear son, co-operate; if you have something else to confess, do so and you will be forgiven."

In that context, Esteban T.'s behaviour not only departed from what was advisable, but also put his weak physical health in jeopardy. Esteban T., affectionately dubbed "the crazy professor," with a fair share of sarcasm which made our physical and psychological survival easier, did not precisely look like a Spartan hero: short, thin, with thick glasses on the hook of his aquiline nose -which gave away his Italic heritage- spent his days wrapped up in his thoughts. The prisoners couldn't remember any previous confrontations he may have had with any of the wardens.

And while the prison warden yelled at him again: "What else, inmate? What else?!!!," shielded behind the thick bars to prevent any physical attack, and becoming increasingly mad with fury, Esteban T. looked at him wondering what could possibly be expected of him. Meanwhile, his fellow ward inmates gave him a mental push so he would complete his utterance with the two magic final words, viz., Mister Warden, which would lead him both to safety and to an answer.

There was deathly silence. One could hear the hissing of the heaters burning gas in the middle of the ward, or in the distance the squealing and screeching of the steel and tin gates opening and closing in other wards.

The prisoners exchanged looks in which one could read both assertions and questions of the kind: "Esteban can stand his ground." "Finally here's one standing up to one of those bastards." "What does he want, to be beaten up?" If he doesn´t answer, he´ll be locked up in the hole and get a good thrashing." With their thoughts came the conclusions at once: "Now we´re all in for it." Our next visit day will be cancelled." "We will have to go without food." "No breaks for a week."

So they all concentrated hard in order to encourage Esteban T. and push him into giving the right answer once and for all, into acknowledging first the title of Mister and then his position as Warden.

Meanwhile only Esteban T. knew of his suffering and effort to solve the puzzle imposed by the warden in such an unfriendly manner. "What else should I say?, What is missing in my request?" hopelessly wondered Esteban T., who had already spent several years in the Rawson penitentiary paying tribute, a hard tribute for his involuntary disobedience of protocol. Like someone who in front of four delicate crystal wine glasses does not know which is the right one for red wine, Esteban T. was at a loss to figure out what was expected of him both by the warden who kept on hollering, and by his mates, who continued to look at him in a funny way with light nods and small mouth openings as if trying to convey a hidden message.

The warden's voice thundered again: "So, Esteban T., what else should you say?" The warden had by now been joined by other colleagues, who, sympathetically standing up for him, peremptorily demanded of the inmate: "Hey you, don't get smart on us and answer properly. You are not getting away with this."

The prisoners mentally asked Esteban T. to give up his resistance, convinced that was the reason why he didn´t conform; asked him to please reconsider and stop putting them all at risk. However, Esteban T., far from having made a pithy decision, and facing all the risks that this implied, still wondered what to do. Those few minutes seemed endless. Suddenly his face brightened up and with a smile on his face, in a very distinct voice, he simply and categorically uttered: "Good afternoon."

They had never laughed so heartily, nor would they ever do so again throughout all their years in prison. There was generalised fearless roaring laughter for a while, without any attempt to suppress it. With tears in their eyes, the prisoners doubled up in pain, while Esteban T., his hands akimbo, looked at them inquiringly behind glasses that slid down and got stuck on his aquiline nose: "So what are you laughing at now?"

# Alternative Therapy

Carlos S., the Rawson penitentiary barber, was not your typical man. Of course not. He showed his hatred towards the prisoners when he cut their hair, but to the feeling of hatred he added a rare curiosity to find out about the life and works of the detainees. He specially wanted to know what they had done to deserve imprisonment.

You couldn't see him around in the wards. He was nearly always in his office and sometimes in some administrative office or other. The prisoners had found him there sorting out files and keeping up records. Just as in a school, which is why he had been rebaptised as "the teacher" by the inmates.

When Carlos S. found out his new nickname, the prisoners knew of his fury because of the roughness he showed during haircuts. "So I'm the teacher for you, eh? Just wait and you will see I'm a real expert/master wielding my tool."

And he would apply himself zealously to his task. He would make the prisoners sit on an ordinary chair and would wrap their neck with an old towel and looking in the direction of the mirror, in which he and his client were reflected, he would say sarcastically and impersonally "I use this towel so that your hair doesn't stick to your jacket. I wouldn't want to be criticised if they come to visit you." Then he would ask, like a ritual, "How shall I cut your hair?" to which all the prisoners would answer according to their taste, knowing beforehand that the cut would be the same, close-cropped, identical.

He had in his power two cutting tools: a pair of scissors for those who came to him with long hair, which was unusual, as well as a manually operated gadget which cut with two blades that he operated from the tips of the handle, which he would squeeze with his right hand. It looked like a lawn-mower: a head with two handles that held and steered it. His cuts would even turn out to be similar: even and radical.

He was a quick man. In every sense of the word. Good barber that he was, he would interrogate his "clients" warning them that they could dispense with the formula "mister warden." "Warden will do."

"Did you go to college/school, inmate?"

"I was a psychology major, but I quit/I didn't complete my degree, warden."

"Why were you arrested?"

"For being a Peronist, sir."

"I didn't ask you about your ideology. What exactly did you do for being put in prison?"

"Well, I was an activist in a poor neighbourhood. I taught adults reading and writing."

He would get excited by this dialogue.

"Have you read *Pedagogy of the Oppressed* by Paulo Freire?"

"Yes, of course."

"And *Education as a Free Practice*?"

"Yes. Do you know them?"

"Here, I'm a barber. But not as ignorant/dumb as you think."

These dialogues, which were usually short, would suddenly end abruptly. At that point Carlos S. would take it out on the prisoner's heads. He manipulated the skulls at his discretion with his left hand: they were *mate* balls when he turned them around by the chin, light bulbs when he took them by the temples and puppets when they were pushed by the neck. The machine would make deep and even furrows which he then trimmed with additional ones which only succeeded in cutting the prisoner's hair even shorter. They ended up looking like raw recruits with crew cuts. In Carlos S.'s conscientious job injuries were not absent. You could sometimes see bruises or even small blood points. The inmates didn't complain. They knew that if they did so the barber's behaviour would be more cruel.

Finally, a touch of sadism. Carlos S. would stand behind the prisoner and raising a small mirror, which he turned around so that the inmate could see the back of his head, he would ask.

"What do you think, inmate?"

"Nice, thank you, warden," mumbled the prisoners, knowing full well that any objection could result in a blow or even worse, an additional haircut on the excuse that he would make it better.

On one occasion towards August of 1977, a new contingent of prisoners arrived at Rawson prison. After going through the usual identification process, the medical check-up and the interrogation by the Intelligence Staff, the detainees were sent to the wards and in the days following they were taken to the barber's office.

Osvaldo B. was a teacher from the Province of Buenos Aires, an honest, straightforward person who had no time to be briefed on how he should behave when dealing with "the teacher." After a few days in quarantine inside the ward, his first day out was in that dreaded place where, at least from the point of view of their hair, they were all equal. "Good morning, inmate."

# Revisiting Her

Alberto P. had waited for a long time, and even if he had been longing to see her again for quite some time, the memory of the hurt it had caused him had paralysed him each time he had tried. But this time his mind was almost made up.

He had lived with her several years, and although other men, whom he knew, had also done so, he did not feel jealous or envious. It even seemed to him that having shared her, the pain had lessened. After all, those before and after him had to endure her just like him.

However, he had never been able, up to this day, to help feeling a strange attraction to her, perhaps precisely because of all the intense suffering. Alberto P. had to admit that he had learned something from her. Without a doubt, he had become a man in the sense that he had learned to hide his feelings, to wait patiently for the hard times to come to an end without falling into despair, and to find a glimmer of light where most could only see shadows.

Finally, and after wavering until the last minute, he was determined to go and see her. It wasn't far, just some five hundred miles away. Early the next morning, he got into his car, went to the gas station and asked: "Fill it up, please, premium. Could you also check the water, oil and tyre pressure?"

"Sure, sir. It's best to be safe when you are on the road."

Since it was a little after seven, his requests were promptly seen to. He paid, left two pesos for a tip, started the car, put on the safety belt, heaved a deep sigh and, holding on to the steering wheel at ten past ten, said to himself in an effort to muster up courage and strengthen his conviction: "Off we go! I should be arriving around two or two-thirty."

Then he added: "I'll be such a surprise for her!"

It was the end of February, and it was very hot. Alberto B. remembered the programme on climate change he had watched on TV the night before. He then turned on the radio to listen to the morning news.

The temperature had now reached twenty-two degrees centigrade. Those in favour of the government and those opposed had got tangled up in an argument about inflation. Hillary Clinton and Obama were still competing in the primary elections, whose outcome was hard to predict. Nothing new, really.

What struck him the most was the news that the instigators and executors of the Trelew slaughter thirty-five years ago were still being arrested? "These murderers must be at least seventy. They will petition for house arrest. These jackals certainly know how to take advantage of a democratic and constitutional state!!" he thought.

Annoyed, he switched over to another station. There were usually lots of folk music programmes at that time. He could hear Horacio Guaraní singing: "Both of us are prisoners, my jailer, me behind bars, you in the grip of fear." After three hours' drive he stopped at a gas station on the crossroads. He was in San Antonio Oeste now. He needed to stretch his legs, get a cup of coffee, and refuel.

"Fill it up, sir?"

"Yes, thank you."

"Travelling far?"

"I'm travelling south. How's I-3?

"In very good condition. Our penguin president has had all the interstate roads in Patagonia repaired. Are you headed for Santa Cruz?"

"No, not that far south."

Alberto B. was in no mood to chat. All he wanted was to get to his destination. He paid and drank his coffee in the station coffee-shop, while he watched the buses come and go past the large windows. As usual, there was a whistling wind.

He got back into his car trying to cheer himself up: "C'mon, Albertito, there´s only a short distance left. If you have made up your mind to make this trip, you now have to have the will to get there."

He drove off. Left and right, the road showed the same scenery: small and flat shrubs, swayed by the eternal wind. Well, not swayed really, but beaten and taken by surprise. He drove on leaving behind a large dried up and salty pool of water, the result of occasional rain and continual evaporation.

He drove past Sierra Grande. He remembered: "Now the Chinese have a concession to exploit the mine." He slowed down, shifted to second, put on the warning lights, turned right and drove into the town. The memory came back to his mind: This is the only place in Argentina where the people have taken over the roads. Some of the housing complexes were deserted. Not a soul could be seen, not even a car. The doors and windows were missing. The frames had been ripped off. He had once heard all the plumbing and piping had been removed, although he could hardly believe it.

He sighed. "Hopefully, one day the people will be able to regain it," he wished to himself, as he got back on the road.

He arrived at the border with the province of Chubut. The clock on the dashboard indicated it was one p.m. Half-suspicious, half-nervous, he looked at his wrist watch. Yes, it´s one p.m.! "We´re fine. She must be having her siesta now. She used to be a stickler for punctuality," he thought.

A road police officer signalled to him to stop. He did so and wound down the window. "Good morning! Welcome to Chubut! Could I see your papers, please? Green card, insurance policy, and driver´s licence."

Alberto B. said good morning and produced the required papers. "Are you driving further south, sir? Work or tourism?"

"Yes, I´m continuing further south. Personal reasons. Just a visit."

The police officer examined the papers, and looked at the car plate. "Very well. Everything looks OK. Enjoy your trip, sir."

"Thanks a lot."

He drove on leaving behind a large dried up and salty lake, the result of occasional rain and continual evaporation, which seemed an eternity to him. He tried to find a reasonable explanation for this. "It's the monotony of the scenery," although he knew that it was the imminence of the meeting that shook his heart. He wanted to get closer, at the same time as he was waiting for an excuse to drive away.

He had not let anyone know he wanted to see her. Perhaps he would not have been granted permission. Besides he wanted to surprise himself, without any concessions after being a part of her for twenty-five years, and to surprise her, of course, so that she wouldn't have any time for preparations.

"It's best without any warning," thought Alberto B, "just like the first time."

He drove into the town. Actually, it was a city now. Nothing looked familiar to him, so that he had to use a map to find his bearings. He didn't want to ask the way; he was determined to get there finding his own way around, going back, losing his bearings, getting lost and finding his way again, but all by himself. Finally he caught sight of her as he drove across a boulevard. Surprised, he could make out her backside, which had always struck his attention, and, like the first time, he was left speechless.

She was tall, as expected, though not as tall as she had seemed twenty-five years before, because he had grown up during that time, and so due to a question of relativity in proportions, it looked as if she had become smaller. Besides, her back, at one time stiff, revealed a certain kind of physical decay; it looked weather-beaten.

Cars as well as passers-by came and went oblivious to his rendezvous.

"At long last!" said Alberto B in a low voice, so that no one else but she could hear.

Unruffled, she did not show any signs of emotion. She remained motionless and unperturbed at his presence.

He drove around her to see her face and arms, those arms that had embraced so many men, and that face which with a smile had seen some arrive, and had sadly seen others leave. Her face, just like her back, and despite the efforts to prevent it, showed the ravages of time. The make-up could hardly compensate for the quarter of a century that had gone by.

Her arms no longer looked so stiff, so strong, so frightening.

Alberto B. stood in front of her. With his arms akimbo, he raised his eyes and told her what he had been waiting to tell her for so long: "I never loved you, although I must admit that I learned a lot about life while I was with you."

Without waiting for a reply, he added: "I don't bear a grudge against you; after all, you are just an instrument for the men in your care."

"I did not desire you," he went on. But I had been longing to see you all these years. I wanted to have this chance, not out of revenge, but because I wanted to pay off and old debt. After all, I stayed with you for five years, rather, *inside* you." Then he remained silent, without waiting for a reply, and stayed there looking at her for an indefinite length of time. Actually, Alberto B. was not sure whether time had stopped or whether it had gone back twenty-five years.

He stayed there wrapped up in his thoughts, until someone in uniform walked up to him, and warned him that this was a security area. "You can't stay here unless you move around. Are you waiting for a staff member or are you waiting to see a convict?"

"No, I'm not waiting. I just wanted to see again the prison where I spent five years of my life."

www.ingramcontent.com/pod-product-compliance
Lightning Source LLC
Chambersburg PA
CBHW060934050726
47592CB00003B/954